PR@2CEO
Presents

Meet The ERs

The Four People You Meet On The Way To The Top

by

Kevin D. Carr

Foreword

by

Tom Izzo

Head Coach Michigan State University
Men's Basketball

Meet the ERs: The Four People You Meet on the Way to the Top

Published by Kevin D. Carr and PRO2CEO, LLC

Note: Exponential Sports and Entertainment (ESE) are fictitious company.

For general information about our other products and services, please contact our Customer Services department within the USA at 347-709-1870 or email info@pro2ceo.com.

The author, Kevin Carr, is the Founder and CEO of PRO2CEO, LLC (www.pro2ceo.com), which is a career transition and business development firm. PRO2CEO offers an array of training and development seminars, speaking engagements and products. Go to www.meettheers.com and www.kevindcarr.com for more information.

ISBN-13: 978-1515286745
ISBN-10: 1515286746
Printed in the United States of America
First Edition: December 2015

To Missy

[signature]

TABLE OF CONTENTS
Page 3

What People Are Saying About Kevin Carr and

The Book Meet the ERs...

"Super cool, very funny read."
—Ne-Yo, Singer, Songwriter, Producer & Actor

"Meet the ERs" draws on the author Kevin Carr's years of experience as a transition and business coach and reminds us that the most successful leaders and organizations in the world govern themselves with values above all."
—Duncan Niederauer, Former CEO of the New York Stock Exchange

"*Meet the ERs* draws on the author Kevin Carr's years of experience as a transition and business coach to some of the most successful people and organizations in the world on how to govern ourselves with values and leadership. *Meet the ERs* is a creative look at how we easily get infected with other people's issues until we learn how to cure ourselves by administering doses of self-identity and personal leadership."
—Tirrell Whittley, CEO & Principal, Liquid Soul Media

"As a professional athlete in the sport of basketball, getting to the top of my game was not easy. The book Meet the ERs has helped me better understand the ERs I may meet on and off the court as I try to learn to be the leader of my own business now and in the future."
—Trevor Booker, Professional Basketball Player and Future CEO

"Meet the ERs is fun, full of attitude and burdened with an undetectable *behavioral* virus going around the workplace. The lead character, Eric, has to figure out how to cure himself of the ERs before he misses out on an opportunity of a lifetime. Go get this book! It could save and accelerate your career at the same time!"
—Melanie Perry, President of Perry Coaching

"*Meet the ERs* does a great job hitting the mark for young and seasoned leaders. The book makes you aware of how we all can be carriers of the behavior virus called the 'ERs' and spread the least effective ERs if we are not careful. The good thing is there's a cure inside this wonderful easy read that we all can learn, grow and benefit from."
—Ben Crump, Attorney & Activist

"I can't recall a more fun parable story told which captures all the creative personalities that can exist within people on the job, a sports team or even within a member of your family, like the ERs. It's a must for those trying to learn the essential soft skills needed to get above the fray and find their place at the top."
—Mo Ager, Former NBA Player and Grammy Nominated Artist

"Kevin Carr, author of *Meet the ERs*, does a colorful job telling the story of a young upstart, Eric, and the competition he goes through with four people he meets on his way to the top. His journey can easily be applied to almost any work-life environment. *Meet the ERs* is a great read for young upstarts and seasoned professionals alike."
—Tracy Ellis-Ward, Assistant Commissioner Big East Conference

"As a retired military veteran, I used to run into behavior with enlisted troops that had to be corrected in training or it could be detrimental to the success of a mission. *Meet the ERs* is a simple way to get today's soldiers and leaders to creatively overcome dysfunctional behavior to improve morale and results."
—Kenneth Carr, Retired US Air Force

"*Meet the ERs*" has it all: humor, personality, and authenticity. The characters

"Churches can be some of the most challenging, but best places to cultivate change. Meet the ERs is an ideal method for any organization to use who wants to address dysfunction and increase more positive outcomes in people."
—Rodney Patterson, Shiloh Missionary Baptist Church

Every current and former athlete has to figure out what special gifts they possess and what they need to do to thrive and not just get-by once the playing side of sports it over. Instead of just giving you warnings, this book shows you the preventative steps on how not to catch the non-positive aspects of the career-derailing virus called "The ERs."
—Kris Benson, Former MLB Player & CEO of Superior Business Management

Foreword

Being the leader of a competitive D1-A Men's basketball team can be much like being the CEO of a major Fortune 500 company. When Kevin Carr told me about his idea to write a book that shows which traits can make or break a person in a team or business environment, I knew he was onto something unique. For almost two decades as an NCAA head coach at the Michigan State University, it has been my role to create the chemistry and team cohesiveness that can transform a group of rookies into a team of high performing veterans. I have coached my share of "Blamers", "Clingers", "Leapers" and "Do-ers." In fact, when Kevin and I worked together at MSU, the basketball team was in the midst of dramatic change. We were going from just competing to becoming national champions. Slowly but surely, we became "Do-ers" in creating a championship environment.

During one of the greatest points in my coaching career, Kevin Carr served as the Player Development/Life Skills Coach. He assisted and offered support when some of my players stumbled and often redeemed themselves on the journey to finding their way to success. His story of the "ERs" resonates in a lot of my players. Eric's journey has many parallels of how people find their way to success both in sports and in life. I found I could even see myself in all of the ERs at different points in my career. The characters may be fictional, but you have met each of these people in some area of your professional or personal life. An easy enough read to reach readers from all walks of life, this could be useful for an emerging young leader because it provides tools and insight when faced with adversity. This book is also great for seasoned leaders and managers who need a fresh approach to coaching the various levels of people they work with. This isn't a book about taking shortcuts but instead about personal growth. It will help you perform at a higher level in order to be that "Do-er" who can turn mediocrity into extraordinary.

"*Meet the ERs*" has it all: humor, personality, and authenticity. The characters have both the strengths and shortcomings symptomatic of anyone on their way to the top.

—Tom Izzo, Head Coach, Michigan State Men's Basketball Team

Introduction

You're probably asking yourself, *who is Kevin D. Carr?* It's a fair question. There are a lot of people who claim to be experts at something or have something important to say. I truly believe I have a unique perspective that can really help people achieve life and career success.

If you follow sports and you're an avid to casual fan, you've seen me. I was Vice President of Social Responsibility and Player Programs at the NBA from 2001-2014. The most visible role I had at the NBA was during the NBA Draft. For ten years straight once a rookie's name was called I provided them with their authentic NBA Draft cap and escorted them to the stage to receive the official handshake from the commissioner. Most people saw this role as inconsequential and mostly for show, but there is much more to it than meets the eye. In actuality, my role was very significant because so many things happen to a player after he is drafted and it's good to have a go to person to help them with their transition into and eventually out of the NBA. In addition, I was there to support families and close friends too because they go through a major transition and it's not just the player who's life will change in many ways.

The NBA is an incredible company to work for. It gave me amazing opportunities to change and impact the lives of players, families, children, and communities overnight with the power of its brand. My role at the NBA was to coach players on all the off-court business obligations of being a professional athlete all while competing at the highest level of professional basketball in the world. I also assisted the NBA in recreating their social responsibility efforts and was part of the team that developed the global outreach program, NBA and NBA-D-League Cares. I had the opportunity to travel the world carrying the banner of social good wherever I went through the great programs sponsored by the NBA league, teams and players. In addition, I helped develop and launch eighteen minor league basketball teams around America for the NBA's Development League.

Of course, a player's transformation from a basketball player to a CEO of a basketball brand does not happen easily. Often the job requires assisting athletes in taking ownership and responsibility of their million dollar brands overnight, and very few players have the experience to do this on their own. Players like Chris Paul, whom I've known since the Nike All-American camps he attended in high school is an example. Hence, the road to success does not come overnight.

While working at the NBA, I was consistently asked the same question: How did you (Kevin Carr) get to the top? After all, working for the NBA is a far-fetched dream for many children. It started like this: Years ago, the NBA took a chance hiring me. I was not the typical applicant. I was not a graduate of an Ivy League school with an extensive resume in professional sports. I was a single parent raised, self-made college graduate from the projects whose reputation and body of work spoke volumes for me. I realized there was a more important answer to this question. I should write a book to share and help others discover how to reach the top of *their* professions. But I did not want to pen any old book about the climb to success. I wanted to create a story compelling and thought provoking, which personified how to manage the group dynamics around you, avoid setbacks, and time wasted chasing opportunities that lead to nowhere. And thus, *Meet the ERs* was born.

I have met hundreds, maybe even thousands, of people through my travels over the past twenty years. At the NBA I had to assess people quickly and determine their needs, whether they were players, coaches, GMs, parents, agents, athletic trainers, owners, team presidents, consultants, colleagues or team staff. The idea for *Meet the ERs* originated from a business trip when I met with a group of professional basketball players. One of our staff members said to the players, "Don't be a blamer, be a do-er." Those words resonated with me. As hard as it may be for people to believe, professional athletes struggle with the same challenges, failures, and insecurities as the rest of us do. So it was no surprise to me that the idea, which birthed Meet the ERs, came from a professional development seminar for pro athletes.

To pass time during my daily three-hour commute to and from work at the NBA, I began to write about the differences in performance, as I saw them, between Blamers and Do-ers. I wrote this book to help people identify what I consider to be four primary behaviors, three of which can wreak havoc and cause major dysfunction in lives and in work environments. If you are trying to get to the next level in your career, this book can help you develop soft and relationship building skills to get there. If you are a seasoned manager or leader, use this book to help you identify areas of opportunity in your team that are directly related to the ERs.

I am excited to introduce you to *Meet the ERs*. It is my hope that you will be relieved to know - you are not alone! Each one of us is susceptible to succumbing to dysfunctions in our behavior. Because although the ERs present an exaggerated, in-your-face view of these behaviors, examining the ERs offers insight into how you can contend with these bad behaviors when they surface. My greatest hope is that you will be encouraged to perform at a higher level in all facets of life because you have met the ERs.

Respectfully,

Kevin D. Carr

Chapter 1

What Type of Professional Are You?

After nearly twenty years of training business professionals and working with athletes at all levels in the sports industry, I realized that there are four types of individuals: Blamers, Clingers, Leapers and Doers. Each one has a unique approach to navigating through life, but only one is consistently victorious. Which one is your *perception* of yourself? Knowing what type of characteristics you share with these four types of individuals will help you successfully get started on the path to success in whatever you strive to do.

Blamers
Blamers have excuses for most of the downfalls in their lives. When circumstances do not transpire the way they would like, they blame others rather than take personal ownership. Blamers have escape mechanisms for almost every hurdle they encounter. They tend to use these as testimonials to justify being unproductive. In truth, what these testimonials amount to is a pile of excuses.

Because they often shift blame, Blamers are unable to clearly analyze their actions. They see themselves as victims and often specialize in self-sabotage. The Blamer impulsively points an accusatory finger at others, which only creates rivals and obstacles that did not previously exist.

Blamers also believe that everyone is out to *get them*. A Blamer might assume others are jealous of them. They may even believe their intelligence, beauty or talent threatens others when they come around. These

BLAMER

assumptions often lead to suspicious and defensive behavior that can ruin relationships. Ultimately, Blamers have a difficult time accepting that their perception of situations may be drastically different from reality.

Because of their reluctance to be team players, Blamers rarely ascend to their desired levels of success, personally or professionally. A Blamer seeks to be the superstar on their own team, basking in the glow of accolades and praise. They ignore the proverbial rulebook, believing

11

that rules or standards do not apply to them. A Blamer would rather take the ball home and play alone than abide by the rules of the system. A Blamer is always looking out for self-interest and rarely considers camaraderie an option. This self-serving approach hurts Blamers more than anyone else and hinders them from experiencing the success they desperately want.

In business, Blamers do not look to their own weaknesses as reasons for not succeeding. If a Blamer is not promoted or relegated to a position of leadership, they might accuse a colleague of being the boss's favorite or blame it on workplace politics. When all else fails, they can always accuse somebody, anybody, or everybody of being out to get them.

The Blamer's modus operandi (MO) is to play the victim. By refusing to recognize their role in problems, they limit their ability to grow emotionally, mentally, professionally and spiritually.

Clingers

Clingers are the people who hold onto the past. They consider what *was* to be the best time of their lives. They harbor nostalgia for the good old days and usually resist attempts from friends or colleagues to move forward.

Clingers are mentally unprepared or unwilling to progress because they thrive on what they did yesterday, last month, or a year ago. They talk about what they did when they were in high school as if it were just yesterday. Clingers define themselves by what they *were*, not by who they are or who they aspire to become. They are comfortable with the status quo. They allow fear to keep them from taking on new challenges. Clingers drive forward while looking in the rearview mirror!

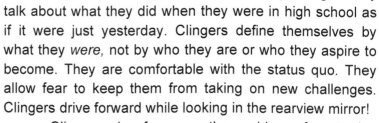

CLINGER

Clingers also focus on the problem of yesterday rather than the solution of today. They vacillate between being paralyzed by past failures and caught up in previous victories. When things go wrong, they tend to spend all of their time rehashing how the dilemma came to be and who set the disaster in motion. The time spent dwelling on the problem could be better spent brainstorming and executing a solution for progress.

In business, Clingers talk about how great things "used to be" when they first started in their position. They relish in letting everyone know how differently the company ran in the good old days. Clingers usually can pull a story from their back pocket about the time when they were the top performer. They are afraid to see the truth and examine themselves in their present status. They fear the realization of how far they *haven't* come, because it's too painful. So, they hide in the past. Clingers press the snooze button on future opportunities and choose to step into their time machines and live in the past.

Leapers

Leapers think they should be further along than they are in their journey. I see Leapers all of the time in business, sport, and everyday life. In sports, it's often the person who thinks they should be the captain of the team, head coach, or manager of the entire operation because they would do a better job. They are impatient and don't see the payoff of paying their dues one play - or one assignment - at a time.

In the corporate world, a Leaper does not see the value of learning at the beginner position. To a Leaper, it feels unnecessary. A Leaper would not last long in the mailroom of a huge corporation; each day would feel like time wasted. This person would look around and resent anyone they perceived as having advanced more rapidly. Leapers don't take pride in entry-level positions. Hence, they would not perform diligently because their attention would be focused on positions well beyond their actual capabilities.

LEAPER

Leapers are notorious for not listening, to anyone. They often exhibit unsportsmanlike (i.e., less than collegial) behavior. As a result, they often burn bridges. Building professional relationships is often an important factor in creating opportunities. Whether on an athletic field or in an organization, "teammates" should be able to learn from each other. No one player knows it all, and even if they did, they couldn't accomplish everything alone. That is precisely why coaches, captains, managers and teams exist. Leapers rarely recognize what they can learn from superiors. In their minds, they already possess all the tools to fulfill the roles they desire.

Leapers are so busy trying to get ahead, get the next job, or beat the next opponent that they often lose focus of their *current* role of being a good teammate. By jumping the gun, they do themselves a professional and personal disservice, and in turn, never benefit from the experience of embracing the process of improvement. Rookie or entry-level positions exist to allow time for grooming and development. Assisting an executive is how a newbie can learn the fundamentals of a career, in addition to the etiquette of the workplace. Leapers often miss these lessons. Instead, they would rather spend their time thinking of how they plan to replace the executive.

Finally, Leapers are unwilling to put in the full amount of time and energy required to make it. They often give up and move on just before a major breakthrough. As aggressive as they are, Leapers often don't get very far as they think they should in most instances at work and in team situations because they lack patience it takes to get to the top.

Do-ers

A Do-er knows how to seize the moment and stay cool consistently. This is a person who focuses on their dreams and seeing how individual goals fit into the big picture of the team's goals. Do-ers know how to prioritize appropriately, and they can be counted on to get the job done. Do-ers in basketball, for example, may or may not lead the team in scoring, rebounds, blocks, or assists, but they consistently prove to be clutch contributors when called upon. Ultimately, Do-ers are the "go to" people.

DOER

Do-ers are considered natural leaders. They are skilled and know how to motivate others to be their best as well. Do-ers are able to grasp the reins of leadership without being entrapped by power. When in positions of influence, Do-ers know how to appropriately delegate. They value experience and have the wisdom to call upon past lessons without living in the past. A Do-er consistently takes on opportunities to be a major contributor in both personal and professional situations and to be an asset to their team, school, organization, and community. Do-ers take personal responsibility for what happens on and off the court. In some ways, they take everything personally. They are very aware of how their behavior, attitude, and character work together to reflect their brand. Do-ers show up on time. They get their rest. They manage what they eat. They take responsibility for their development in areas with or without management or coaching. A Do-er understands that even when

14

advancement is achieved, there is always room for growth. A Do-er's lifestyle is built around the concept of self-improvement.

Do-ers are self-disciplined professionals who strive to go the extra-mile. They understand there will be obstacles along the way, but they do not act from a place of fear. In order to move forward and experience growth, Do-ers face challenges head-on with the intention of prevailing. They have mastered the art of capturing the moment, using it for progress and moving forward with heightened skill. Do-ers give particular focus to the journey, not just the destination.

Whether you're an athlete, an aspiring researcher, an emerging entrepreneur, or in the stages of reinventing your career, you can probably identify with one of the ERs, either personally or through someone you know. Admittedly, over the course of my personal and professional life, I have been each of these types. I was commended for being a "Do-er" as a newcomer on the job for my ability to discern and make prudent decisions. When I interned in college, I was recognized by department-heads because I put 100% into every task they assigned me. Who wouldn't want to "cling" to such praise? After college, I remember wanting to make the "leap" from broke student to well compensated director! When advancement didn't come as quickly as I had hoped, there were times when I yielded to the temptation of "blame." Thankfully, I soon learned timing is everything, and patience and persistence were my allies. I used every experience to my advantage.

Through my years of experience I've also learned the workplace can be a breeding ground for contagious, infectious germs. They lurk everywhere, on keyboards, telephone receivers and door handles. Co-workers carry them around, cough, and sneeze them into the atmosphere just in time for the next employee to walk right into the pathway of the icky microorganisms floating in the air. Before long, someone else has caught it—whatever *it* is.

The ERs are contagious, infectious, and transferrable; the good news is, they are completely avoidable. Just like a cold, the ERs can spread into an epidemic, but they also can be evaded by conscientiously exercising preventative measures.

You may ask yourself, "How do I know if I've caught the ERs?" After all, most people rarely detect when they are infected. At first glance, it may not be obvious one of the ERs has been encountered. They are often well hidden and cleverly disguised. The symptoms are not always as obvious as a runny nose. They often reveal themselves in the things you say and the way you handle daily situations in your professional and personal life.

The ERs refer to sets of behaviors that can *make or break* situations in almost any area of life; they can have an effect in sports, politics, school, personal relationships, non-profit and the corporate world.

Chapter 2

Meet Eric

Eric is an apprentice at Exponential Sports & Entertainment (ESE), a top agency for obtaining major endorsements for athletes, artists and entertainers. Once a decent college basketball player himself, Eric got a shot at a pro tryout but did not make it to the league. He finally realized he needed to transition from sports and knew it was time to get his professional working career going. Eric's apprenticeship was a great opportunity to do something in an area where he had a high interest and passion. Eric experienced the pervasiveness of the ERs firsthand as he was charged with working with several different people in his new position. Meet Eric as he gets acquainted with The ERs.

The first day on the new job was a bit overwhelming for Eric. He wanted to dress to impress his new bosses, so he wore the suit his parents bought as his college graduation gift.

ERIC Eric appreciated them investing in his future. Now that he nailed the interview and received an offer to be an apprentice at a prestigious agency, Eric was eager to show them a return on their investment. He took one last look at his reflection in the massive glass building and stepped through the revolving doors.

Although he was early, Theresa was already there to meet Eric in the lobby. She was his new boss's assistant, and Eric recognized her immediately from a few weeks before during his initial interview. Her smile was genuine, and it made him feel a bit more at ease as they shook hands.

"Good morning, Eric. Welcome to Exponential."

He returned the greeting and she led him toward the elevators. Once inside, she began giving him so much information, he felt like he should be taking notes.

"I'm going to have you work with one of our smaller, but nimble teams to start. The team members are Brenda, Carl, Larry and Daria. You will have an opportunity to work with each one of them individually, and I think you can learn quite a bit during your time with them. Today, I'll start you with Larry, our junior account executive. He's our newest exec so his account list is a lot lighter than some of the others."

Eric looked up at the florescent numbers ascending on the elevator LCD. It showed they had reached the sixteenth floor and were still climbing.

"You are scheduled to meet with Larry for lunch today. He came from another company last year. He is pretty experienced in the industry. In addition, I want you to sit with Carl. He knows everything about the company, and I do mean *everything*. If you have any questions throughout the day, jot them down and ask Carl later. I'm sure he can answer them."

They were now at the twenty-third floor and still climbing. Theresa turned to Eric and gave him a reassuring smile.

"This is a fast-paced environment, and you'll have to wear many hats, so I hope you're ready for the ride. Mr. Malone says you graduated near the top of your class and really impressed him because you accomplished this while competing as a student-athlete in college. We're hoping to see great things from you."

She nudged Eric in a way that she thought was encouraging, but everything she said made him want to burst free from the elevators and run! All this was so new to him. There was a lot riding on this position. Mr. John Malone, the president of the company, was an influential man with connections all over the globe. If he thought Eric was worthy, then there was no room for error. Eric would have to prove that Mr. Malone's instinct was right. He'd have to perform like a winner.

Eric gulped nervously one last time as they reached the 30th floor. The elevators opened slowly to what he could only describe as complete chaos. Suited men and women rushed about yapping on cell phones and clutching tablets under their arms. The rows of cubicles seemed endless. Theresa moved to the right, but Eric wasn't fast enough and was almost run over by a guy his age pushing a mail cart.

"Excuse me," Eric muttered, embarrassed.

The mail guy looked at him as if he was thinking, *Watch where you're going, rookie!* Eric picked up his pace to keep up with Theresa who, although a foot shorter, walked with the quick step of someone who was on an urgent deadline. A few curious people glanced his way, and he noticed his suit paled in comparison to most of their clothing. So much for trying to impress.

Theresa made so many turns that Eric was sure he'd never find his way back to those elevators. Finally, they reached the office where he remembered being interviewed. Sure enough, Theresa knocked once and pushed open the door where Mr. Malone sat behind a gigantic desk talking on the telephone. On his desk sat a couple of pictures of his wife and children, a lamp, a mahogany nameplate and one portfolio. Mr. Malone held up his index finger to indicate he'd be finished with his call in a moment. Theresa stood waiting patiently, so Eric did the same. He glanced around at the awards and plaques decorating the walls.

Three minutes later, Mr. Malone ended the call and turned his attention to Theresa and Eric. He motioned to the leather chairs in front of his desk.

"Eric, glad you could join us at Exponential today. Have a seat. Thank you, Theresa."

Eric sat slowly as Theresa exited the office.

"Good morning, sir," he said, "I'm glad to be here."

Mr. Malone, a distinguished man in his mid to late forties with wisps of gray hair near his temples, smiled pensively.

"I'm glad to hear that Eric, because I just received a phone call about a great opportunity for our company. We could use your assistance."

Eric sat up straighter.

"Of course, how can I help?" he asked.

"I take it Theresa already explained a bit about how you'll be assisting my 'Dream Team?'"

"Dream Team?" Eric asked in confusion.

"That's what I call them," Mr. Malone explained with an amused smile. "This is the group Theresa has booked for you to do your rotation with at Exponential. They handle a large percentage of our athletic endorsements. Larry is a fairly recent hire, so he provides a fresh new perspective and has already displayed the ability to quickly accomplish objectives. Carl is the most experienced team member. He has a wealth of knowledge and is a great resource. I think of Brenda as the ethical

19

barometer of the team. She isn't afraid to slow the process, if necessary, to ask questions and ensure that we are doing things the right way. I think you'll really like Daria. She is consistently efficient and extremely productive."

Eric nodded while taking mental notes of the qualities Mr. Malone valued in his team.

Mr. Malone continued, "The "Dream Team will be working on securing a marketing plan for Cody Brooks."

Eric almost choked. *Cody Brooks?* This was one of his favorite ballers, one of the rising stars in professional basketball. Eric had followed Cody's career since high school, all through college, and into the pros.

"Wow…sir…that's *amazing*," he managed to say.

Mr. Malone smiled a knowing grin, as if he knew that would get Eric's attention.

"There are a few deals on the table, the typical stuff, a sports drink endorsement, a breakfast cereal, maybe an underwear ad."

Eric could sense that Mr. Malone wasn't exactly ecstatic.

"Sir, that sounds…great, to say the least…but I sense that there's a problem."

Mr. Malone nodded his head in agreement.

"You sense right, Eric. The problem is that Cody Brooks is a very challenging to place right now as a client. He's not easily pleased or sold on any of these deals we have found for him. In fact, he is considering no longer working with Exponential. This is where the Dream Team comes in. If I could get one of my executives to secure a national endorsement for a client of this magnitude, it could mean big things for us at ESE. They will need your assistance around the clock."

Eric swallowed nervously. First day on the job, and he could feel the weight on his shoulders.

"Are you up for some long days and nights, Eric? I need your full commitment."

Eric nodded in a way that he thought looked enthusiastic instead of terrified.

"I'm up for the task, sir."

*On Eric's first day, before he even has a chance to digest the overwhelming, fast-paced environment of the company, he realizes he will have to prove himself. He will have to work with several people to ensure that they have what they need to succeed. He is fully aware that his success is directly connected to their success.

Chapter 3

"I should be CEO"

After his meeting with Mr. Malone, Theresa escorted Eric to his cubicle. It was pretty standard, a small gray space that held a desk on which sat a computer, stapler, office cell phone, and a huge bottle of hand sanitizer. Eric could see that others spruced up their cubicles with family photos and greeting cards. All he could think about was calling his dad and his friends with the news that he would be working on a marketing campaign for Cody Brooks. For a second, it crossed his mind to keep it to himself. If this Dream Team that Mr. Malone discussed was unable to secure the deal, there would be nothing to brag about anyway. It all depended on this group of executives.

"What's up with the sanitizer?" Eric asked, pointing towards the oversized bottle next to his computer.

"Oh, that," Theresa sighed. "We are doing a Healthy Hands Movement throughout the building. Something has been going around that we just can't seem to eliminate. Fourteen people on this floor alone called in sick this month."

Eric's eyes widened a bit. "That's crazy," he said. "It must be highly contagious."

Theresa nodded emphatically, "Yep, seems like just when one person gets better, someone else catches it. You just make sure *you* don't catch it, okay?"

Eric pumped a bit of sanitizer into his palm as a precaution.

"Let me show you the supply room so you can settle in," Theresa said, pulling him from his thoughts.

Eric spent the morning stocking his desk with sticky notes, pens, highlighters, and all the other office knick-knacks he would need to stay organized. Before he realized how much time had flown by, it was time for lunch.

"Hey, you must be Eric," a voice said, startling him.

Eric looked up to see a man in his early 30s reaching over the gray wall of the cubicle to initiate a handshake.

"Oh, yeah...hi," Eric said, pulling himself together. He accepted the handshake, which was firm and confident.

"I'm Larry," the guy said loudly as if Eric should already know. "Theresa said you're joining me for lunch. You ready, buddy?"

Eric closed his desk drawers and stood slowly. He was ten years old the last time someone called him "buddy," but he decided not to point it out.

Larry chose the restaurant, not bothering to ask Eric's opinion. He chomped down noisily on chips from a humongous metallic bag even though they were on their way to lunch. He also talked loudly during the five-minute **LARRY** car ride, running down his lengthy list of past positions at other companies. Not once did he ask Eric about himself. In fact, Eric wasn't sure Larry even came up for air.

"I mean, I don't like to toot my own horn," Larry said, parking the car, "but I'm the most experienced guy on my team. I've worked for every marketing firm in a 20-mile radius, so if you want to learn from somebody who's seen and done it all, I'm your guy!"

"That's good to know," Eric replied, "I was hoping to work with someone who can show me different aspects of the business."

"Oh yeah, buddy, absolutely!" Larry said through a mouthful of potato chips. "You stick with me and I'll take you along for the ride to the top. Don't worry - when I'm 'CEO Larry Rhodes,' I won't forget the little people." He winked his right eye to confirm his point.

He nudged Eric playfully with his greasy hand and led the way into the restaurant.

Once inside, Larry chose seats at the bar, which Eric thought was strange. He silently hoped Larry wouldn't actually order a drink. Luckily, Larry ordered an iced tea, which he finished in three huge gulps.

"So have you thought about going into management?" Eric asked, figuring the best thing to do was to ask Larry about himself, since that appeared to be the focus of his conversation.

Larry sighed in an exasperated way, as if he was relieved someone finally said it.

"It's crazy you should ask that, because I really already should be in management. I mean, I've been in this business so long!"

Eric watched as Larry reached into the basket of warm bread the waiter sat between them. He began devouring it as if it was his last meal.

"Did you start as an apprentice like me?" Eric asked.

Larry looked up from the bread and his menu as if Eric just said the craziest thing he'd ever heard.

"*Apprentice?* Well, I tried that once for a few weeks. It wasn't for me," he said. "No offense, buddy, but I don't understand the point of working without getting paid. I just don't get it."

Eric chuckled to show he was good-natured. "That's one way to look at it," he said, "but if a person wants the experience and knowledge…"

"Hey," Larry interrupted through cheeks full of pumpernickel, "I get the whole *idea*. I'm just saying that it's never been for me. I prefer to get experience under my belt and money in my pocket at the same time."

Eric decided to let the issue go. He could see there was no getting Larry to see the bigger picture. They ordered their lunch entrées and ate. Well, Eric *ate* while Larry practically *inhaled* his food. Larry continued to discuss why he would be better for management. Eric nodded and listened, unable to get in one word.

While meeting with Larry, Eric notices that the best way to handle a person like this is to let them do the majority of the talking. Larry would rather hear himself talk than listen to the new guy. People who lack the ability to take turns during a conversation typically do not build strong interpersonal relationships. Unfortunately for them, building rapport and professional relationships are skills essential to advancement. Being a good listener is a quality most employers, coaches, leaders, and everyday people look for when making connections. Even people who are dating often say that being a poor listener is a "deal breaker." Larry is unaware he has caught this condition, but his terrible listening skills are a symptom of his infection. He is now incapable of seeing the value in a colleague like Eric and Eric's position. After all, from Larry's perspective, Eric is just an apprentice, so he sees Eric as unimportant. If anything, Larry thinks Eric is foolish for taking an unpaid position. He fails to see the full value in learning.

- *Have you ever worked with someone who is a big talker, who rattles on about themselves?*

- *Do you know someone who never sees the bigger picture because their tunnel vision is focused on what they want?*

- *Have you ever turned your nose up at a potential opportunity because you were not receiving instant gratification?*

Chapter 4

"Back in My Day"

Back at the office, Eric exited the elevators and turned the corner to find a middle-aged gentleman in a frumpy, outdated suit and navy tie sitting on his desk.

"Uh...can I help you find something?" Eric stammered.

The gentleman did not stand, but he picked up a pyramid-shaped paperweight on Eric's desk, turned it around and around in his palm and did not say anything for few seconds.

"So, you're the new guy, huh?" he asked finally, bringing his eyes up to Eric's without blinking.

Eric did not want to appear intimidated, but this guy seemed menacing! He wondered if this was Mr. Malone's boss or someone even higher up the ladder. Whoever he was, he was pretty audacious, sitting on Eric's desk with his scuffed up shoes resting in his chair. He looked at Eric as if he was daring Eric to tell him to move. Eric decided not to comment on the foot on his chair, even though keeping quiet made him feel like he was allowing this guy to walk all over his turf.

"Yes...I'm Eric Woods. I just started today. And you are...?"

"Dobson," the man said. "Carl Dobson."

So, *this* was Carl. The executive who had been a part of the company long enough to see management change seven times.

"Oh, Mr. Dobson...it's great to finally meet you," Eric said, sticking his hand out impetuously.

Carl did not reach out and shake Eric's hand. He stared at it for a moment before placing the paperweight in Eric's palm.

CARL

"Call me Carl," he said, crossing his arms over his middle. "Heard you went to lunch with Larry."

Eric nodded.

"Yeah, Mr. Malone wants me to do a short rotation with each of you and Larry's schedule was open today. When would I be able to shadow you, Mr. Dob- I mean, Carl?"

Carl frowned a bit and sighed as if he was bored. Eric watched as he dropped his dusty shoe to the floor. He pumped a bit of Eric's hand sanitizer and rubbed his hands together slowly as he maintained his steely glare.

"Look, kid," he began, "I've seen so many apprentices come and go, I wouldn't be able to count 'em if you paid me."

"Well, my plan is to stick around for the long run," Eric said boldly.

"Sure it is," Carl said almost sarcastically, "but the business isn't what it used to be. Management isn't what it used to be. These days, if you want to get ahead you have to make quite a few friends and enemies. You know, you kids call them "Frienemies." Nobody gets ahead by shadowing anymore. No disrespect to your American Dream idea, kid. You might even have what it takes, but that isn't the way through the doors to success in this building."

"Even still," Eric said, "I'm sure going to try."

Carl looked amused. He stood up and straightened his wrinkled suit jacket.

"I used to be a rock star like you, kid. Wanted to be the top exec and have my name on plaques all over the office walls. And it was. But the business just isn't like that anymore. But if you want to follow me around and create a few spreadsheets just to prove you've got what it takes, be my guest."

Eric watched Carl's back as he walked away coolly.

Most people have encountered a "Carl" in the office place, the person who has lost all ambition, is convinced the corporation is on a downward spiral and each man should be looking out for self. These people have experienced their fair share of highs and lows. Carl probably does not intend to give a negative impression; he is simply comparing his present environment to what he remembers from the past.

When he first encounters Eric in the cubicle, Carl props his shoe on Eric's chair to mark his territory. Think of the people you have worked with who find ways to announce how they have been with the company practically since the beginning of time. Sometimes they are unaccommodating because they may feel threatened by a new presence. It is common for these individuals to take a while to warm up to "newbies." New employees represent change, and that can be vexing for a long-termer like Carl. He is showing some moderate signs of being a Clinger, but the jury is still out on this one.

Being Carl's shadow is exactly what Eric did for the majority of the afternoon. He stapled Carl's loose papers, filed contracts and spreadsheets and answered his phone. He didn't understand why Carl was so disgruntled. Theresa said that Carl knew this business like the back of his hand. What Eric noticed most was how Carl's complaining went on throughout the afternoon, spilling into his business calls and even a phone call with his wife, during which, he ran down a list of everything anyone did to annoy him on this particular day.

"Hey, kid," Carl said, glancing over his shoulder, "check my email and flag anything important."

Carl wasn't particularly computer-savvy. Eric noticed he jotted information down on sticky notes and used an old-fashioned pocket calendar instead of the electronic one built into his desktop. Carl mentioned earlier how much he despised email and social media. He said, more than once, that business people formed real relationships back in the day. When they had something to say, they walked over to the person and just said it. Eric predicted the majority of his assisting Carl would be reading his emails.

Carl's inbox included the typical subjects, such as lunch meeting confirmations. Eric continued to scroll past all the messages Carl did not bother to open. Suddenly, a bubble popped up in the right-hand corner of the screen, alerting Eric that Carl just received a new message. The subject read "Cody Brooks' Shocking Arrest." He clicked on it and a news article appeared.

"Hey, Carl, you might want to read this," Eric whispered to Carl's back.

Carl did not turn away from his phone call.

"Read it for me, kid, and update me later with the important details."

When Eric clicked on the news article, the first thing that popped up was a full photograph of Cody Brooks in a nightclub, looking slightly

28

inebriated. He held a long frosted bottle of alcohol in his one hand and used the other hand to form a "peace" sign for the cameras. Eric skimmed down the article to find out the nature of the charges against Cody, silently hoping that it wasn't a felony or something that would hurt his career in a way that would make it impossible to work with him. After all, Mr. Malone made it very clear the firm needed clients with Cody Brooks' celebrity power.

The article read, *"Cody Brooks, who is being considered as a candidate for Rookie of the Year, was arrested on charges of assault and battery after leaving Pandora's box, an area nightclub last evening. Mr. Brooks and his entourage engaged in a physical confrontation with unnamed partygoers at approximately two o'clock in the morning. Mr. Brooks is suspected of striking William Collins over the head with a glass bottle. Collins was admitted to Community General Hospital where he is listed in fair condition. Mr. Brooks has been released on bail."*

"Not surprised," Carl said, startling Eric. He didn't realize Carl had ended his phone call and was reading over his shoulder.

"What do you mean?" Eric asked.

"I mean that Malone just pulls anybody onto our accounts. This Brooks kid could be bad for our brand. He's part of this new social media age. He thinks he can do whatever he wants, posts it on one of those online sites, and still use us to get rich. Back in the day, clients didn't act like that. And neither did executives. We combed through potential clients with more scrutiny. We were more selective. It wasn't just about the almighty dollar."

"I think Malone wants the best for all parties involved," Eric said diplomatically.

Carl chortled in a way that made Eric feel foolish.

"Keep believing that, kid. Keep believing in fairy tales. When Greenwich was here, that's probably the last time I saw someone in management really try to build an authentic, genuine infrastructure at ESE. And that was decades ago."

"Greenwich?" Eric asked.

Carl ran his hands over his shiny salt-and-pepper hair and interlocked his fingers at the nape of his neck.

"Yea, Bart Greenwich. He was my manager back when I first started at Exponential. Now that was a guy who knew real potential when he saw it. That was a guy who knew how to lead a team."

"You don't think Malone is a great leader?" Eric whispered.

"He's all right, I guess. But Greenwich...I was top account exec of the year each year I worked under his lead. We were unstoppable, kid."

The verdict is in—Carl is afflicted with being a Clinger.

Carl Clinger refers to his successful past, but that success cannot continue to flourish unless he is willing to make moves and changes. Sometimes just having an open mind about the concept of "change" can create positive results. But Carl Clinger wants things to stay the same.

If the desire is to climb to higher altitudes in life or career, one cannot afford to approach change with reluctance. Imagine how much faster Carl Clinger could generate results in his profession if he embraced technological advances. Imagine how much more equipped and empowered Carl could be if, instead of griping and groaning about having to take on something new, he viewed these occasions as adding something to his "tool belt." Carl Clinger clings to the past instead of embracing the present and all it requires, and as a result, he disempowers himself every time he needs an apprentice or assistant to handle the aspects of his job he did not add to his professional tool belt of skills.

- *Have you ever felt like your ambition in your professional life has dwindled away with time?*

- *Do "newbies" make you feel like your position is threatened or are you able to welcome new people into the fold?*

- *Have you ever been the person resistant to evolving with changing times and circumstances?*

Chapter 5

"It's Not My Fault"

"Talking about the dark ages again, Carl?" someone said jokingly.

Eric and Carl looked up simultaneous to see a thin, wiry woman with slightly disheveled hair leaning over the partition of Carl's cube. She grinned at them mischievously.

"Don't you ever get tired of the age jokes, Brenda?" Carl asked with a slight smile. "When are you going to get some new material so I can actually laugh?"

Brenda laughed and held her hands up innocently.

"Come on, Carl. I'm trying to take it easy on you, old man. Don't want to hurt your feelings. I know how sensitive you can get."

Carl sighed like a teacher giving up on a pupil. "This is why you never finish your work. You spend too much time stalking me. Back in my day, kids like you didn't last two seconds in marketing."

Brenda frowned as if she was genuinely wounded. "How can I finish when a new account gets dropped on my desk every other day? Look at this list of stuff they want me to do by Friday!" she exclaimed, waving a sheet of paper in the air. She crumpled it up dramatically and rambled on.

"I was handed three more accounts last week and nobody gave Larry one. What about you, old-timer? Anybody throw grunt work in *your* inbox?"

Carl didn't bother answering. Eric got the feeling this was a regular conversation between the two.

"Maybe our new apprentice can help you since you can't seem to keep up," he said snidely. "This is Eric."

"Hey," Brenda said. "Welcome to the team."

Eric nodded back and hesitantly reached out to shake Brenda's hand. He didn't want to be rude, but he was still reeling over Theresa's tidbit of information about the office virus. The last thing he needed was to get sick right when it looked like he could be getting a big break in

BRENDA

his career.

"You meet anybody else on the Dream Team besides Grandpa here?" Brenda asked.

Eric glanced at Carl before answering.

"Larry took me to lunch earlier."

Brenda looked peeved. "See what I mean?" she said. "I get this crazy mountain of work and everybody else gets the newbie before me. If anybody needs the help, it's *me*."

"Should I take out my violin now or later?" Carl joked.

Brenda tossed the crumpled piece of paper she was holding in Carl's direction before storming off.

The next morning, Theresa added "Organization with Brenda" to Eric's calendar. Eric thought it might mean he would learn tips about organizing in the office from Brenda, but when he stepped into the cubicle he could not believe his eyes. Brenda had not been kidding; her desk looked like it had been struck by a typhoon.

"Wow," Eric said, letting his mouth hang open.

Brenda turned her chair around swiftly to see what Eric was talking about. "Oh, hey, Eric," she said.

Choosing his words carefully, Eric said, "This is some clutter you've got going on here."

Brenda squinted her eyes for a second and looked around as if trying to assess whether the situation was as bad as Eric made it seem.

"Well, if they'd stop putting new stuff in my inbox, I could sort this old junk," she said defensively. "I mean, what sense does it make to give me all of this? I've got a new baby at home. I'm the *last* person who should get the overload."

"I didn't know you are a new mom. Congratulations. And I'm here to help." It was then that Eric realized what Theresa intended for him to do. "We can get this in order in no time. Where should I start?"

Brenda immediately shoved a pile of folders to the side of the desk where Eric stood.

"I guess you can file this stuff. We're at the end of the fiscal year, and I want to make room for all the new jobs that will get thrown onto my desk in the coming weeks."

Just as Eric pulled up a chair to begin sorting, Theresa rushed over.

"Meeting in the conference room now," she whispered to the both of them.

Eric watched her back as she rushed off in another direction. Every time he saw her, it seemed she was in a hurry.

"Well, we've been summoned," Brenda, said in a mocking tone as she stuffed a pile of papers into a drawer.

"I'll see you in there," she told Eric. "I need to grab another cup of coffee and call my husband back."

"Oh, but Theresa said it's an emergency," Eric said.

Brenda waved him away and picked up the receiver to her desk phone as she said, "Yeah, yeah, I know. The world won't come crashing to an end if I'm a few seconds late. Trust me, I probably won't be the only one."

Eric hesitated before hurrying away. He grabbed a notepad and pen from his own cubicle on the way to Mr. Malone's conference room. He hated to leave Brenda behind, but he figured it would not be the smartest move to show up to one of Mr. Malone's meetings late.

Carl and Larry were already sitting at the long table, along with a guy not too much older than Eric. Across from them sat Mr. Malone and a serious-looking man who watched Eric's every move as he scrambled to find an open seat. The room was silent as Theresa slipped through the door and eased it shut behind her. She took her place beside Mr. Malone, pushed her glasses up onto her face, and gave him her undivided attention.

Mr. Malone was his usual no-nonsense self. He neither smiled nor frowned. His eyes never lingered on any one person for too long. This was a man who had mastered the art of commanding a room without having to even open his mouth.

"I called everyone in this morning in light of the new press on Cody Brooks," Mr. Malone began. "I thought this would be as good a time as any to introduce you all to Mr. Brooks' agent and to start formulating a game plan on how we can work around these recent developments."

Mr. Malone gestured to the man on his left.

"This is Jack Sullivan. He's here to ensure that we are on the same page as Mr. Brooks' PR team—"

Mr. Malone was interrupted by Brenda, entering the room while attempting to balance a steaming cup of coffee, a notepad, and her tablet. No one looked over at her except Mr. Malone, and his eyes were on fire. Brenda eased her way behind others and slipped into an open chair next to Eric. After a moment of awkward silence, Mr. Malone continued with his introductions.

"Jack, this is the marketing team I have enlisted to work on Cody's endorsements, Carl Dobson, Larry Rhodes, Brenda Baker, Daria Young and our apprentice, Eric Woods."

Everyone exchanged pleasantries, but Eric could still feel the tension in the room. It was obvious that Jack Sullivan had arrived to oversee damage control. If he felt the Dream Team couldn't keep Cody Brooks' chances at major endorsements intact, then it would be Jack's job to find a firm that could.

Jack cracked his knuckles, creating an intimidating sound that blared in the silence of the room.

"I trust everyone here has read the latest development in Mr. Brooks' dilemma," he began. Everyone around the table nodded as if he'd asked a question.

"We all know this is not the first go-around. Mr. Brooks has a knack for creating *controversial* press."

"However," he continued, "we all have a job to do. My job, which recently became a bit more challenging, is to land Mr. Brooks the most lucrative and beneficial athletic contract possible. Your job is even more complicated. Your job is to ensure that he lines up endorsements regardless of how likeable or unlikeable he is in news blogs and social media."

Eric wondered if anyone else in the room felt like Jack Sullivan was asking the firm to make the impossible possible.

"This latest incident is probably the most detrimental of all Mr. Brooks' recent incidents," Jack went on. "He was lined up for commercial advertisements with Prolific Protein Bars and B.I.G. Energy Drinks. Both endorsements have been pulled."

Brenda's mouth hung open. Carl looked up at the ceiling as if he was not surprised. Larry looked at his watch as if he was late for something. Daria, the one account executive Eric had yet to meet, jotted notes on a small notepad.

Mr. Malone chimed in, "I have spoken with representatives from both corporations. They don't seem to be budging on this. So, while Jack works overtime with Mr. Brooks' PR team, we need to work overtime finding new endorsements to replace the two that were retracted."

"Mr. Brooks is giving your firm six months to deliver," Jack said. "After that period of time, if the endorsements are not on the table, he will be ready to move on to another firm. Any questions?"

Eric looked around the room at the executives. Larry was the first to speak up.

"I don't want to be negative," he began, "but if Cody— I mean, Mr. Brooks, does stay in the media for an extended period of time, how realistic is it for him to be the face of *any* commercial advertising right now? Have we considered the option of Mr. Brooks serving out his time or doing a significant amount of community service hours and us revisiting this arrangement at a later date?"

It was a valid question, one Eric had thought of too, but didn't feel bold enough to ask.

Jack smiled slowly and said, "Rest assured that Mr. Brooks will not be spending any time behind bars."

That wasn't even an explanation, but everyone around the table accepted the response at face value. Carl spoke up next.

"Don't you think the results would be more favorable if Mr. Brooks showed up himself and was present during our crusade for him? He's not even here today. I mean, if I shop him around to different companies and he doesn't even bother to—"

"Mr. Brooks is a very busy man," Jack interrupted. "A pro athlete of his caliber cannot be present at every meeting that is held on his behalf. His presence needs to be on the court. However, I will run it by him and see if his assistant is able to find openings in his schedule for a meeting or two, but I cannot promise it will happen. Next question."

Brenda raised her hand as if she were a student in school. Jack gestured for her to speak up.

"You're just looking for two deals, right? I'm asking because we have four execs here working on this, and I already have a pretty heavy account list, so if—"

"That sounds like a personal question for me, not for Mr. Sullivan," Mr. Malone interjected.

Embarrassed, Brenda stared down at her tablet and jotted a few notes.

"I have a question," Daria said, taking the cap off her pen.

Eric finally got a good look at the fourth executive, who like Brenda, looked to be in her early thirties. She was smartly dressed in a charcoal suit and white blouse with her eyes fixed on addressing Mr. Sullivan with her question.

"I think I speak for the team when I say that we want whatever deal we can procure to be a good fit for Mr. Brooks and for him to feel comfortable with his name attached to that brand. Are there any particular endorsement categories where he would prefer us to direct our focus?"

"I'm glad you asked," Jack said. "I would say, Mr. Brooks is particularly interested in deals regarding electronics, athletic clothing, and health foods. Stay away from vehicles and absolutely no fast food."

Eric watched everyone around the table scribbling notes on paper or typing them into their smartphones. As Jack stood to his feet, everyone else around the table followed suit and stood hesitantly. Jack went to shake Mr. Malone's hand and was interrupted by Theresa.

"Uh, uh…one moment, sir," she said. Theresa held out a bottle of hand sanitizer and squirted a bit into both Jack's and Mr. Malone's hands.

Jack chuckled, "Oh, I forgot. Healthy Hands, right?"

Back at Brenda's cubicle, Eric tried to shake off the weight of the impromptu meeting, but he could see right away that Brenda was practically bubbling over.

"You okay?" he asked, frowning at the way Brenda paced around the area near her desk.

Brenda looked up suddenly as if she didn't expect Eric to be standing there.

"Eric, don't you get it? They are expecting us to do something that can't be done! No company is gonna want to spend their marketing dollars on an athlete with an unresolved incident lingering over him."

"Cody Brooks?" Eric asked. "I don't see why not. He's a pretty standout athlete."

Brenda shook her head and then thumped her index finger against her temple.

"You're not *thinking*. You have to think like a marketing exec, not a basketball fan. Due to his latest off-the-court issue, the general public may feel this Cody is not being responsible; especially with the great opportunity he has before him to represent a brand. His antics are great for the social media or the paparazzi, but they aren't great for what Malone expects us to do."

Eric shrugged, "Brenda, some clients are easy to work with and some are more challenging than others, right? Isn't that the nature of the business?"

Brenda leaned down so close that Eric leaned back in his chair.

"I think Malone is trying to move people around big time," she whispered, "and I predict a bunch of people will be getting a one-way ticket out of here. I'm no conspiracy theorist or anything, but something doesn't smell right about this whole deal."

Eric did not respond in fear of contributing to Brenda's illogical rant. He did not want to fuel the fire that was already ablaze.

But it was too late. Brenda straightened her suit jacket angrily and stormed out of the cubicle back toward Mr. Malone's office. She felt like if no one else had the guts to speak up against what was clearly an insurmountable task, then she would do it. It wouldn't be the first time she spoke out against what she considered to be an injustice.

How a person reacts to inadvertent circumstances reveals a lot about their character. Let's face it - things don't always play out as planned. In the corporate world, mergers happen, demotions and promotions occur, companies liquefy and disperse, and through it all, people have to find effective ways to cope. Job responsibilities differ. Some require heavy travel; some include inconsistent pay, and some offer challenges that vary from day to day.

It is human nature to wonder why more work or different types of work are given to one employee and not others in linear positions. However, Brenda Blamer has complete control of her reaction. She chooses to complain and hint at unfairness, and it is obvious this is a pattern for her. Brenda Blamer could change her perspective. If she is, in fact, getting more work than her colleagues, she could view this as a sign that management sees her as more capable, responsible and perhaps more equipped to handle larger accounts. Instead, Brenda Blamer spends her time protesting. Her focus is on blaming others.

While she complains she is buried in work because of being overloaded, she wastes time joking with Carl and griping to Eric instead of using her time to be a top performer on the job. She justifies being late for Mr. Malone's meeting because she has to return a call to her husband and refresh her coffee. Brenda's agenda and victim mentality impede her professional responsibilities. Notice when Eric questions her decision not to leave for Mr. Malone's meeting immediately, Brenda Blamer's excuse is that she probably would not be the only one late. The professionalism, or lack thereof, of others should never affect one's own professionalism. Eric manages to dodge catching this symptom when he chooses to leave Brenda Blamer behind and get to the meeting on time.

When Jack Sullivan opens the floor for questions, Brenda has excuses and even seems to be establishing a way to get out of being involved with the project. After the meeting, Brenda Blamer becomes suspicious someone is "out to get her." Her immediate response is to make quiet accusations about backhanded schemes for which she has no proof.

- Do you respond to adversity in a self-destructive way?
- Do you search for someone to fault like Brenda Blamer?
- Do you view unexpected changes and challenges as sabotage by your coworkers, or are you fearless and accountable enough to face changes and challenging situations head on without looking for scapegoats?

Brenda Blamer is not the only identifiable ER in the meeting with Jack Sullivan. There are hints to identifying the ERs in each person's communication during the meeting. Larry Leaper asked a question about abandoning the plan to work with Cody Brooks altogether. His inquiry is inappropriate because it is a suggestion fit for the boss! Larry Leaper, an account executive, attempts to leap into the seat of the CEO. Larry Leaper should make a suggestion aligned with a contribution he can make that fits the situation. In addition, his suggestion about shelving Cody Brooks on the backburner shows he is not a team player, an obvious symptom of being a Leaper. Larry Leaper does not think for a second how a decision of that magnitude will affect the entire team. He clearly does not want to inconvenience himself with a difficult client and tries to do Mr. Malone's job.

Carl Clinger's personal feelings about how executives and clients should do business make him sound old-fashioned and ornery. Does it really matter if Cody Brooks is at the meeting or on a conference call listening in? His manager, the person responsible for representing him is there. This is a common practice and should be enough to satisfy Carl. Carl's preoccupation with how business should be conducted based on his history is symptomatic of him being a bonafide Clinger.

Daria, on the other hand, takes the opportunity to ask a productive question. She may have had strong personal feelings around the subject, but she puts them aside. She recognizes this meeting with Jack Sullivan is simply the presentation of the problem. She stays solution-focused and asks a question that could benefit the entire team. Doing so redirects the meeting back to finding ways to alleviate the problem. Gathering relevant information that will help her do her job more effectively is what makes her a Do-er.

Chapter 6

"That 'No' Sounds Like a 'Yes'"

The following day Theresa informed Eric Mr. Malone wanted him to shadow Daria on one of her local sales calls. This would be a great opportunity for Eric to observe the negotiation side of the business firsthand.

"So, let me give you a little background," Daria said while driving. "Act Fit has been looking for an athlete spokesperson for some time now. They typically go more in the direction of tennis, track, and other individual outdoor sports. Cody Brooks would be a stretch for them."

Eric was confused. "So, why even shop his name there then?" he asked.

Daria smiled and stopped for a red light. "That's the point. My job is to broaden their minds and expand their

DARIA business. We're not selling Cody, we're selling the *idea* that Act Fit athletic clothing is for anyone who admires Cody based on his work ethic, despite his youthful mistakes as a young athlete."

"Oh, I get it!" Eric exclaimed.

Deep down, Eric did not entirely "get it," but he was curious to see how Daria would attempt to change Act Fit's demographic perspective using Cody Brooks' recently re-tarnished image!

When they pulled up to the Act Fit offices, an executive assistant led Eric and Daria to an upper-level suite. The marketing directors were waiting in a spacious conference room. Introductions were made. Eric was a bit nervous, but he noticed Daria was cool and collected. Daria looked like she sat in meetings of this magnitude and gave multi-million-dollar presentations every day.

"Act Fit is a brand that makes people think of wholesomeness, the All-American athlete, the boy or girl next door who wants to be comfortable while breaking records and earning titles," Daria began.

She stood before a presentation screen, and Eric watched in amazement as visual images popped up reinforcing what she was trying to convey. There was an image of a teenage girl playing tennis in Act Fit wear, and then hugging her coach who appeared to be her father. There was a man jumping a hurdle on a track in Act Fit wear, and then holding up a medal around his neck as his wife and small children stood around him beaming. There was even the Act Fit logo draped with the American flag.

"So, I know what you're thinking," Daria went on. "You're thinking, what in the world is wholesome, All-American and apple pie about Cody Brooks?"

There were a few acknowledging nods and even a chuckle or two around the room. They were relieved Daria said it before they had to break the news to her.

"The recent press surrounding my client has not been favorable. I'll be the first to admit it," Daria said solemnly. "Let's go ahead and confront the obvious. He's young, he's at the height of his career, and he did not make the best decision regarding this recent incident. And yes, the world is watching."

Eric looked up at the screen of Cody Brooks standing on the basketball court mid-game with a grimace on his face. Then, numerous pictures of him partying surrounded by partygoers, driving in his luxury car and yelling at paparazzi. The images flashed quickly, too fast to stare at for long. Still, they left the intended impression of Cody as a guy with some issues. Eric did not want to look around the room. He wondered why Daria was digging this hole for herself.

"The operative word is 'young.'"

A few people around the table looked puzzled. Daria flipped to a photo of Cody grinning for the camera like a small child at a community relations event. Then she shared another of him kneeling on a basketball court after making the game-winning shot surrounded by his teammates patting him on his back for his heroics.

"And the reason his being young is important is because it means there is time for him to reform. Cody Brooks' problem is not that he doesn't perform on the court. He *absolutely* performs. He's a spectacular athlete. The problem is his up and down behavior. He needs improved guidance and to learn how to conduct himself with better consistency."

A few people in the room sat up a bit as if they were catching on to Daria's point. Eric wasn't, but Daria was so compelling he couldn't wait to hear her speech come full circle.

"Act Fit is not about being the best, winning the gold or taking the title. Cody Brooks can act like that. Through your brand, Mr. Brooks can transform himself from bad party boy to praiseworthy, all while dressed in your logo. He can give the world an image of reformation through this corporation. If Cody Brooks can do it, then so can anyone. Be admirable and dress like a winner in Act Fit athletic wear. Thank you."

Being a Do-er is about making the best of each moment. The scope and scale of the moment may change. The circumstances will vary, but at the heart of the Do-er is the desire to create win-win scenarios. There are people whose careers have crumbled because of recessions, lay-offs, and companies being bought and sold without warning. These people had to choose between wallowing in their misfortune and identifying opportunities, such as going back to school or starting their own businesses.

Daria is a Do-er because she knows she is up against a company that will never take a second look at an athlete like Cody Brooks. Nevertheless, she helps them to see Cody from a different perspective. She does not give up or cancel the meeting. She does not attempt to gloss over Cody's reputation by pretending it is not an issue. She acknowledges the problem and presents a solution. The most central aspect of being a Do-er is having a solution. Problems will arise. Some of them cannot be stopped any more than one can stop the sun from rising and setting. When a Do-er is faced with what seems like the impossible, it is time to create possibilities.

- *Where can you discover opportunities in the muck of things?*

- *Are you able to keep your momentum when the uphill climb becomes more difficult than you anticipated?*

- *What positives can you find in the middle of a personal or professional storm?*

Chapter 7
The Outbreak

Based on Daria's presentation, Act Fit was willing to give Cody Brooks a chance. They were skeptical in the likelihood of a young, professional athlete like Cody making, what they viewed as, tremendous changes in his lifestyle and habits. As a result, they scaled down the numbers Daria suggested. The negotiations went back and forth for so long, Eric wanted one side to cave so that they could get back to the office and strategize. Eventually, the reps from Act Fit made the compromise. The stipulation was if Cody got into anymore legal trouble through the duration of the endorsement dates, the deal would be off and Act Fit would be reimbursed a prorated portion of their paid endorsement fees.

When Jack Sullivan returned a few days later with Cody Brooks and his bodyguard, Eric almost fell out of the chair in his cubicle, leaning to get a good look. Cody wore a trendy suit with custom sneakers. The music coming out of Cody's headphones was so loud, everyone could hear it as he walked through the hallway. Theresa led the group toward Mr. Malone's office, walking with her usual hurried steps. As soon as the office door closed, everyone outside began congregating in different areas to whisper about what was going on. The water cooler and break room were on fire with chitchat.

"Did you see his sneakers?" Eric heard Carl say as he stepped into the break room. "It looked like he was wearing lime green marshmallows on his feet. I bet that outer space footwear costs more than all my shoes put together."

"Well, it wouldn't be hard considering you're wearing the same shoes from two decades ago," Brenda joked as everyone looked down at Carl's dull and outdated footwear.

Carl was not offended. He simply rolled his eyes and sipped his coffee while several muffled guffaws broke out around the room.

"Why aren't we in that meeting anyway?" Larry asked as he paced the room. "We're the ones working on this account."

"You already started working on it?" Brenda asked.

Larry frowned, "Yeah, haven't you?"

"Where would I find the time, Larry?" Brenda asked. "Your pending list is almost empty. Of course you can line up meetings."

"Here we go again," Larry said. "Stop the pity parade. Your list is longer because you've been here longer. I just got here a few months ago."

"Touché," Brenda responded, "But I still think there are too many people on this account. I mean, who are we working for here, the Dalai Lama?"

"For once, I agree with you," Carl said. "I like having my own accounts. I've always had my own. With all of us on the same account, it makes it a competition, and this business used to be about marketing companies competing against each other, not the execs from the same firm competing. It's backwards."

"What's wrong with healthy competition?" Eric asked.

The three of them all turned simultaneously to stare at him in a way that made him feel like he had three heads.

Just then, Theresa peeked into the break room and whispered that it was time to join the meeting. Silently, Eric and all of the executives made the trek across the sales floor to Mr. Malone's conference room. Theresa introduced everyone to Cody and then took her seat next to Mr. Malone.

"So, we've been discussing the Act Fit endorsement with Mr. Brooks," Mr. Malone began, "which Daria nailed for us. Let's give her a round of applause."

Everyone clapped politely.

"I know the rest of you are still working hard, trying to land meetings and negotiate numbers. I am positive your hard work and diligence will pay off. I brought you all here today because Mr. Sullivan and Mr. Brooks would like to reward you with a token of appreciation. Theresa!"

Theresa stood and handed Eric and each of the executives an envelope. Inside each was a game ticket, in club seating, to see Cody play.

Because the League suspended Cody Brooks for three games for the club brawl, the Dream Team had to wait a week to redeem their tickets. Carl and Larry tried to act like it was no big deal, but once they were all sitting in the plush club seats at the arena, their excitement was evident. Mr. Malone was invited to sit courtside, right next to Jack Sullivan. Although the game was action-packed, Eric couldn't help but notice that Cody did not play the entire first half. He was not a league All-Star like a few of his legendary teammates, but he typically got *some* floor time in the first half. Eric wished he could hear what was being said between Jack Sullivan and Mr. Malone, who were deep in conversation, but they were sitting too far away. Eric turned his attention to Cody where he sat on the bench. Even though he didn't have one drop of sweat, he had a face towel wrapped around his shoulders. He wore a facial expression that appeared nonchalant, but Eric could tell that it was forced. Beneath it was something else, but he couldn't think of a word fit to describe it. Was it defiance? Frustration? Resentment?

Finally, halfway into the third quarter, the coach put Cody in the game. At first, the team suffered two turnovers by his hands, and Eric wondered if Cody's frustration over having to wait so long to play was getting the best of him.

In the middle of the fourth quarter, when a member of the opposing team continued to hand-check Cody, Eric could see his control wane to emotion. He racked up two fouls within a ten-minute period. To add to that, opposing fans continuously booed Cody every time he lined up for a foul shot, most likely because of the bad press he had recently generated. A few fans of the opposing team held up signs that mocked his recent run-ins with the law. At one point, Cody stepped up to the free throw line and it seemed the entire arena was booing him. Instead of ignoring it, he looked up, winked cynically and did a long pause before attempting to shush the crowd by making two free throws. They really went crazy then, shouting unkind words at him. Eric wanted to cover his eyes; it was almost unbearable watching the evening unfold.

"Why do I have the urge to boo him, too?" Carl muttered under his breath.

Eventually, Cody ended up missing both of his foul shots and the game ended with Cody's team losing.

The following Monday, Eric showed up at work full of energy and excited to learn more. He had already made his buddies insanely jealous when he told them about the club seat tickets from Cody. It wasn't like he knew Cody Brooks *personally*. Even when the tickets were handed out, Cody acted too cool to talk to any of the execs, choosing to communicate primarily through Jack Sullivan. But just the fact that he was working on Cody Brooks' account was exciting to everyone who knew Eric.

He strolled into the office, pausing briefly outside the elevators to use the fancy, high-tech hand sanitizer dispenser Mr. Malone had installed in communal areas throughout the building the previous week. Two more people were out sick and it didn't seem like this virus was going away. Some people were taking extreme measures by wearing the white medical facemasks while in the office.

"Buddy, my main man!" Larry yelled out as Eric turned the corner by his cubicle.

Eric smiled and greeted him, even though he was groaning inside. Larry only conversed with Eric when he wanted someone to do his dirty work. He brushed him off several times when Eric asked about shadowing him on sales calls. If it wasn't filing, answering his phone or making copies, he didn't want to be bothered by Eric, who he still called "buddy" or "the apprentice."

"How was your weekend, man?" Larry asked as he shuffled things around on his desk until he found a half-eaten protein bar. He peeled back the wrapper and took a huge bite. Eric notice he was *always* eating and figure it was nervous energy.

"Oh, it was—"

"That's cool," he interrupted. "Look, I need you to make copies of some spreadsheets and historical files for me and bind them real nice so I have some flashy, glossy, high-class looking booklets to hand out at my presentation today."

The very last thing Eric wanted to do was to stand by the binding machine all morning. Those things were time-consuming and required absolutely no brainpower.

"Aw man, Larry, I wish I could, but I have to sit with Carl and one of his clients today."

It was not an overt lie because Carl had told him he could sit in and take notes, but they hadn't finalized an exact time for the meeting. All Eric knew was that it was taking place today. He just didn't know how else to say no to Larry.

Larry looked annoyed for a second, but then his eyes lit up. "Hey, do what you gotta do. You know the assistant who sits over by the break room? Redhead? Skinny? Coke bottle glasses? Send her over to me. I hope she knows how to use the binding thing-a-ma-jig."

Eric sighed and sat his things down in his own cubicle before going to find the sales assistant. He felt terrible sending her over to Larry who didn't even know her name and treated anyone in a subordinate position like a servant.

Carl was easy to find. In the mornings, he usually stood in front of the coffee machine reading the directions aloud and squinting at the levers and buttons in confusion. It always made Eric chuckle to himself.

"Why do they make these things so darn complicated?" he grumbled, when he realized that Eric was standing there.

"Good morning to you too, Carl. Do you know what time the reps from Audio Flex are due in?" he asked.

Carl didn't look away from the coffee machine. Eric watched as he pushed a few buttons until he finally programmed the appliance to percolate.

"There!" Carl exclaimed loudly as if he had made a major discovery. He finally looked over to where Eric stood patiently.

"Nine o'clock, kid."

Eric entered the conference room at 8:58 to see Carl already waiting with his notepad and pens lined up like the first day of school.

"You're late, kid," he said.

"It's not nine o'clock yet," Eric exclaimed, checking his watch.

"You never heard the old saying that 'being early is on time and being on time is late?'" Carl asked.

Eric didn't answer. He eased into the seat next to Carl and powered on his electronic tablet.

"What do you do when that thing crashes?" Carl asked.

"Excuse me?"

"I'm saying...when that electronic gizmo freezes or breaks and you need your notes right away, what do you?"

Eric knew this was going to be one of Carl's lessons about "back in the day," so he didn't take the bait by defending his tablet.

"You're right, Carl. I've never thought of that."

Carl smiled smugly and looked satisfied with his lesson of the day for the younger generation.

Just then, Theresa escorted two gentlemen into the room. They were dressed in casual collared shirts and slacks. One of them carried a large cardboard box, which he sat atop the table. Carl and Eric stood to greet them.

"Mr. Nakamura, Mr. Cruz, we're so glad you could join us today," Carl said, "This is one of our interns, Eric Woods. He's sitting in today for enrichment purposes."

"Let's get right into it," Mr. Cruz began, "After you met with us in our office last week, we really started thinking about how cutting edge this could be."

"Cutting edge?" Carl asked in a puzzled tone.

"Yes, definitely. We read the news. We know Mr. Brooks' 'young-gun' reputation. He's viewed as the kid who experienced some hardships growing up, but made it out of the urban city and now is an emerging star in the league. And we know as recently as last night, he was in an altercation. We were thinking we could use that."

Mr. Nakamura opened the box he'd carried in and pulled out a few smaller boxes of headphones. Eric watched as he retrieved the headphones and laid them out across the table. They were pretty flashy, lined in chrome and painted in metallic jeweled tones like ruby red, emerald green and sapphire blue.

"Our product is not your everyday audio wear. This Audio Flex line is called The Owl. Did you know an owl can detect not only the location of its prey but the direction in which its prey is headed?" Mr. Cruz asked.

"I did not," Carl said.

"Yes. An owl has a sophisticated sense of hearing that can pick up different frequencies at a heightened level because of the asymmetric design of its ears. Our product is similar. It is light years ahead of the competition. When we designed the packaging and look of the model, we went all out. Go ahead, take a look."

Carl and Eric each picked up a pair of headphones and looked them over. Eric was pretty impressed, but maybe not as fascinated as

Carl, who stared at them as if he were looking at equipment from outer space.

"The individual who wears The Owl model is not the everyday kid. He is wise because our product goes beyond simply being aesthetically pleasing. Our user has an appreciation for tone, frequency, and for the technology our product uses to eliminate feedback and sound bleeding. The price bracket is elevated because this product is intended for the individual who spends time in the studio making music or, like Cody Brooks, can afford to splurge on all the bells and whistles The Owl has to offer."

Carl sat down the sapphire-colored headphones and looked through his notes.

"How do you expect my client to market this? What angle are you taking? Just a flashy celebrity?" he asked.

"Precisely," Mr. Cruz said without hesitation. "Along with Mr. Brooks, we have lined up deals with a hip-hop artist and an eccentric socialite known for keeping the party going."

Eric raised his eyebrows in surprise. It seemed counterproductive for the client to feed off the bad-boy persona that was creating so much negative press. Especially since his agent was working with him on restructuring his image. This product-marketing proposal was in direct conflict.

Carl sighed and sat back. "I like where you're going with this, gentlemen. Let's talk numbers so I have something to present to my client."

"Eric," Mr. Cruz began, "Why don't you take these headphones and pass them out to the members of your team while Mr. Dobson and I negotiate."

Eric knew what that meant. The financial side was none of his business. He gathered his tablet and the box of headphones before heading toward the door. Right before it closed, his eyes met Carl's for a second.

Eric may not be feeling it yet, but it looks like he could be carrying one of the symptoms of the ERs. With germs, it's possible to be a carrier and pass them onto others. This is essentially what is happening with Eric. His interactions and exposure to Brenda Blamer, Carl Clinger, Larry Leaper and Daria Do-er may be causing him to exhibit certain characteristics without him being aware of it.

When Larry Leaper tries to get Eric to create binders for him, Eric becomes evasive. He should say to Larry, "I can't do it now. I need to prepare for a meeting. I should be able to do it later today. When I do, I can show you how the binding machine works so you're not stuck in the future when you're trying to meet a deadline." This would help Eric avoid feeling like a pushover and it would demonstrate how he values his time. At the same time, Eric would empower Larry so he would not have to manipulate people to help him in the future.

When Eric arrives at the conference room and is called out by Carl for not being early, what does Eric do? He makes an excuse. He does not say, "You're right, Carl. I should be early to show my professionalism." Instead, Eric says, "It's not even nine o'clock yet." His very first instinct is to defend himself. This sounds like a symptom of the Blamer.

Eric isn't the only one picking up symptoms from others. Carl is clearly infected with being a Clinger, but in this particular meeting, he shows signs of coming down with other afflictions.

In order to develop professionally, teamwork is a chief skill that must be exercised even when working alone seems more enticing. Mr. Malone put together a team, his Dream Team. The idea is for all four executives to work together. With the legalities of Cody Brooks' case, it is pretty clear his image needs to be managed. Carl Clinger is not looking at the bigger picture. Landing an account that celebrates all the things Cody Brooks and the executives are working to eliminate is a selfish move.

Larry Leaper is getting sicker by the day. His interpretation of his current position is getting cloudier and cloudier. Larry wants to be the top boss so badly he abuses his position over his subordinates. After working together for a couple of weeks, Larry still does not know Eric's name. His inability to build rapport and develop healthy relationships amongst his coworkers is only making his job more difficult. Taking the time to make connections and build bridges is paramount to success. It should be done not with the end in mind, but because you genuinely want to get to know your colleagues. The more you know each other and "shoot the breeze" in the morning or on breaks, the easier it is to work together and develop mutually beneficial relationships. Larry has only mastered the art of being a taker. He doesn't have an interest in feeding Eric's hunger to learn the business: He doesn't have an interest in investing in a professional relationship with him. His only interests seem to be related to how he can use Eric to get what he wants when he wants it. People are more likely to offer help when there is mutual respect and they feel appreciated for their contributions.

- How can you better acknowledge your own shortcomings and rectify them in your professional life?
- Are you able to make decisions for the betterment of an entire team or do you exhaust all your energy on your own agenda?
- Where, in the workplace, is it possible to build genuine connections and show camaraderie?

Chapter 8
Where's the Honor?

A video clip of Cody Brooks bumping and exchanging words with a member of an opposing team during a game had gone viral. By noon, there were parodies of the video circulating. Tensions around the office were high. Daria's client, Act Fit, was threatening to pull the deal. However, she reminded them to view this as part of the transformation process. Transitioning his image from negative to positive wouldn't happen overnight. On the other hand, Carl's client, Audio Flex, was ecstatic. The more issues Cody Brooks had in his personal life off the court, the more press he received. More exposure, good or bad, translated into more celebrity power.

Brenda had not made any deals yet. Instead, she sat muttering about conspiracies throughout the day. Larry, on the other hand, had a few potential clients on his list. He stuffed a colossal pile of paperwork in Eric's arms to file each day for a week. Eric wanted to scream until he realized this was the only way to learn from Larry. Unfortunately, Larry Leaper was never going to take the time to teach Eric anything. So, Eric took it upon himself to comb through Larry's files in order to see how he did business. One thing was for sure; Larry did very little business on his own. From what Eric could see, he researched other marketing firms, some of them his past employers, and stole their ideas. In addition, while sorting through and organizing the drawers of Larry's desk, Eric found countless cover letters and resumes for management positions at firms like The Bionic Sports Agency and Skyline Sports, direct competitors to Exponential.

"Let's go, intern, I mean apprentice" Larry said, pulling Eric from his witch-hunt.

Eric abruptly shut Larry's desk drawer and followed him toward the elevators. They were headed to a lunch meeting for Staminator Protein Bars who already had an endorsement deal with Yuri Knowles, a professional football player represented by one of Larry's old firms.

"Your job is to take notes, *lots* of notes, buddy. I can't write and talk at the same time. So hey, you do the writing, and I'll do the talking,"

Larry rambled on through a mouthful of a muffin he seemed to have pulled from nowhere. Eric said to himself, "there goes that nervous energy thing again."

"Also, you don't ask questions. I ask questions. You don't make comments. I make the comments. You hand out the binders, and like I said, take notes."

Eric stared at the descending numbers inside the elevator. They were a perfect indication for how he felt, like his energy and drive were descending slowly down to nothing.

Larry was getting crumbs everywhere, but he kept eating and talking at the same time. "The client, Vincent Pruitt, is a real pain. He thinks he knows everything. He tries to low-ball everybody, but I need this commission. So, if he throws out some ridiculous number, wear your poker face, apprentice. Don't look excited or impressed or anything that's going to make you look like an amateur."

They exited the elevator and hurried toward Larry's car. He pushed the remote on his keychain and the locks chirped.

"It's open," he said as he jumped in.

Eric hesitated, trying to figure out how he was going to open the door with a mountain of Larry's paperwork in his arms.

Larry let down the window and said, "Today, apprentice."

Balancing the files under his chin, Eric eased the passenger door open and slid inside. Larry took off before Eric closed the door completely.

Inside Larry's car, Eric saw a countless number of empty potato chip bags, candy bar wrappers, and other evidence of his binge eating. It was a wonder he wasn't overweight. Larry pulled a bag of trail mix from the glove compartment and periodically poured some into his mouth as he drove. Eric tried not to stare.

The office for Staminator was not far, or maybe Larry just drove fast. Eric noticed he ran a red light, but decided not to point it out. Vincent Pruitt's assistant met Larry and Eric in the lobby and escorted them into the marketing office.

Mr. Pruitt greeted them without a smile. "Welcome. Please, have a seat."

Eric thought his accent made him sound sophisticated, but his tone and demeanor registered as no-nonsense.

"I brought some numbers with me today," Larry began hurriedly. He reached his hand out for the first file, and Eric fumbled putting it in his hand.

He slid a paper in Mr. Pruitt's direction. Pruitt stared at Larry for a moment before looking down at the document. Eric felt like his heart would beat out of his chest. Mr. Pruitt waved over his assistant, whispered something in her ear, and she rushed out of the room.

"Is this a joke?" Mr. Pruitt asked.

"I'm not smiling," Larry responded.

Pruitt smiled with his mouth but not his eyes. Then he reached inside his suit jacket and took a pen out of his breast pocket. He scribbled something on the document and slid it back in Larry's direction. Eric's eyes darted toward the paper as a reflex. He knew it was private, but he had to see those numbers. *Two million dollars?* Eric could not imagine negotiating that amount of money. Larry looked at him, and he looked away quickly. Larry held his hand out for the next file, which Eric placed in his hand more steadily this time.

"I took the liberty of compiling a few charts for you. Now, the first one may look familiar. It's the decline in popularity of your product over the last three years. They're not *my* numbers. I just do the research." He shoved the paper across the table, but Mr. Pruitt did not touch it.

"This next document shows the decline in popularity of your top sponsor, Mr. Yuri Knowles, and of his team." Larry slid that paper in Pruitt's direction also.

"Lastly, this document shows the *increase* in popularity of my client, Mr. Cody Brooks. The chart is broken down by television, news, game sales, surveys and polls, and online buzz. See, Mr. Brooks doesn't need your protein bar. You giving him this money is really a favor to you."

Next came a long, almost unbearable, silence for Eric. Mr. Pruitt tapped his fingertips atop the table for a while. Eric could see Mr. Pruitt despised Larry, but he also saw something else in Pruitt's eyes: defeat.

The way Larry treats people is directly connected to his impatient nature. Everything he does is rushed, from the way he drives to the way he eats. He cannot bear to wait for anything. To him, his instructions to Eric are not meant to be rude. He just cannot risk "the apprentice" messing up what he hungers for so badly. He does not have time to walk Eric through the ins and outs of the negotiations, so he brings him along to carry files, hand files, take notes, and listen.

Leapers tend not to take the time to conduct business with integrity. Their sights are on the end goal, not the journey or the processes involved in getting them there. Larry Leaper has created so much bad blood, he's leaving bodies alongside the road with every business move. He does not think about, or seem to care about the fact that he might need support when he reaches the peak. How will he stay there if he has not conditioned himself to be a fair, honorable comrade?

No one trusts Larry Leaper because he has not taken the time to cultivate trusting relationships. In his business meeting with Mr. Pruitt, Larry doesn't negotiate. As a result, he does not create harmony and misses the opportunity to have Mr. Pruitt feel his decision to take the deal is a win-win. Instead, Larry makes Mr. Pruitt feel as though he has been beat.

- Do you try your best to create win-win situations for yourself and your professional associates?

- Would others consider you to be fair in your professional dealings?

- Can you count on others to support you in future endeavors based on the way you have conducted business with them in the past?

Chapter 9

Conspiracy Theories & Whistle Blowers

In the weeks that followed, tensions in the office simmered until they practically bubbled over. Mr. Malone announced his Regional Sales Manager was retiring from the company, and he was looking in-house for a suitable replacement. This caused some executives to become a bit more ambitious, while it made others more stressed. Eric worked closely with Brenda for an entire week, helping her sort out which clients should be at the top of her priority list and which could be passed on to an entry-level executive. Brenda felt like she couldn't outshine the competition until she got rid of the unnecessary fillers on her client list.

"I heard Larry is shopping his resume around," Brenda whispered to Eric as they combed through her files.

"What do you mean?" Eric whispered back. "He's leaving?"

"He's being Larry. He's lining up a better position just in case Malone doesn't promote him."

Eric frowned, "How do you know?"

"I know a lot of things," Brenda bragged.

Eric wanted to ask more questions, but he didn't want to be a gossiper. However, he did wonder how Larry was able to job-hop every couple of years. Leaving didn't make sense to Eric. There was only one promotion available and at least fifteen interested candidates. Eric figured either Larry must be exceptional at his job, or he knew many people who opened doors for him elsewhere whenever he did not get his way.

"Did you know sometimes when Larry is claiming to be on a sales call, he's really interviewing with other companies?" Brenda said.

Eric did not want to buy into what Brenda was saying. As a matter of fact, he wished he hadn't heard it. "That's crazy," Eric said simply.

"I'm just telling you what I heard."

"Hearing it doesn't make it true," Eric retorted.

"You don't need proof. Larry takes his briefcase to lunch with him."

"Maybe he conducts business with his clients during lunch," Eric suggested.

"It's never on the schedule. If he was doing business for Exponential during his lunch, Theresa would have it on the calendar. All sales calls are placed on the electronic calendar so we don't step on each other's toes."

Eric hated to think Larry was fraternizing with other marketing firms in hopes of solidifying a position elsewhere, or worse yet, deliberately stealing business from his colleagues. Nevertheless, after seeing how Larry bullied clients to tip the scales in his favor, Eric wouldn't necessarily be surprised to find out that any of this was true.

"What are you saying, Brenda?"

Brenda responded, "I'm saying his client list is so impressive because he doesn't put the business on the books until he has investigated who the rest of us are pursuing. Then, he swipes them out from under our feet. The Staminator deal was on my prospective list. It's a bit of a coincidence that he nailed them without anybody even knowing he had a meeting lined up."

Eric wanted to ask Brenda why her prospective client list was so easily accessible. But he didn't waste his time. He already knew the answer to that question. Brenda was one of the most unorganized people he'd ever encountered in a workplace. She misplaced things so often, it was common to see her ripping her desk apart only moments before an important meeting. Several times Eric approached Brenda's desk to find she had left her email open and personal files exposed for all to see. Even though stealing others' ideas was unequivocally unethical, Brenda's naiveté and lack of attention to detail didn't help the situation.

"Don't you think Mr. Malone would notice that kind of foul play?" Eric asked.

Brenda scrunched up her face as if what Eric said was the most foolish thing she'd ever heard. "Are you kidding?" she whispered harshly. "Malone cares about the dollar signs on the books. He doesn't care whose putting them there. I heard Larry's dad and Malone go way back. I think they attended the same university or something. That's probably how Larry got this job. It's not like he's a star performer. He takes long lunches and he's late everyday—"

Before he could catch himself, Eric blurted out, "So are you."

Brenda stuttered over his response for a moment. "Yeah, yeah, but I...I just got married, just had a baby, I'm renovating my house...I have valid reasons. What's Larry's reason? He lives alone in a building and has a maid and a doorman. He comes in late and leaves early. At least I stay later to make up for coming in late in the morning."

Eric didn't respond. Clearly, Brenda's promptness, or lack thereof, was a sore subject, and he did not want to create bad blood between them. They worked quietly for the majority of the morning. At one point, Eric looked up to see Brenda surfing the net for nursery furniture, completely ignoring the email bubbles that popped up in the corner of her screen, alerting her to new messages.

Brenda Blamer spends a great deal of her time keeping track of what others are doing wrong. None of this time is used to reflect on her behavior and on how she could improve herself. Brenda Blamer has a laundry list of suspicions about Larry Leaper, and what does she do with this information? She gossips about it with the apprentice.

Since Blamers tend to think everything is a conspiracy, they can get downright paranoid when the stakes are high. In Brenda Blamer's case, the opportunity for promotion has brought out the worst of her characteristics. She does not see Larry Leaper misuse company time, but she shares invalidated information with Eric as if it were true. She does not know Larry Leaper's father personally, but insinuates to the nature of his connection to Mr. Malone as if she has first-hand knowledge.

Whenever office gossip spirals out of control, it is typically a Blamer who sets it in motion. Pointing the finger at someone else can be exhausting and time-consuming. Brenda Blamer spends so much time investigating Larry Leaper, she neglects the business on her own desk.

- *Where do you spend the majority of your energy in the workplace?*
- *Are you careful of what you repeat to your work acquaintances?*
- *Are you the careless "whistle blower" people seek out when they want the "goods" on someone?*

Chapter 10
Hidden Opportunities

Mr. Malone called a meeting later in the week to discuss the open position in greater detail. Everyone filed into the large conference.

"As you all know, Vince Shubert is retiring later this month."

Whoops and cheers resounded around the room. A few people patted Vince, a middle-aged, stoic-looking man, on his back.

"The person who takes over this position will have enormous shoes to fill. Vince has been a staple in this company for many hrs and has made great contributions to the success of the firm. I'm looking for someone who is hungry to succeed and is a critical thinker who can think outside the box to make business happen."

A few of the executives sat up straighter because they believed Mr. Malone's was describing one of them.

"One thing I did not previously reveal is a second opportunity for advancement within the firm. When I promote an executive into the manager position, it will leave an opening for a new account executive. My goal is to fill that seat with one of our very own apprentices or assistants."

Eric's jaw dropped.

"Account execs, your job over the next month or so is to really work closely with our assistants and apprentices. Feed them the knowledge that was fed to you. Prepare and groom them to have what it takes to fill an executive seat."

Eric glanced at the members of The Dream Team. Carl looked bored as he softly drummed the pads of his fingers atop the table. Larry looked at his watch and readjusted his tie for the millionth time. Brenda tried not to look exasperated, but Eric could see the frustration over having to take on an additional responsibility in her eyes. Daria jotted notes, as usual, as Mr. Malone offered more details.

"My expectation is for the entire team to work together for the benefit of the firm. This is greater than any one individual. So as you leave this room to strategize and formulate plans, keep in mind, *teamwork makes the dream work.*"

Mr. Malone's announcement means Eric's opportunities are greatly increased. When he first joined the company, the opportunity was simply to learn and gain a wealth of experience by working closely with professionals who had already reached a certain level of success. When unexpected chances like this arise, many people approach them from an emotional place. They may think about why they are the most deserving or they may get overly excited thinking about what perks come along with such a promotion. This is a risky approach. The best thing to do is to focus on self-improvement. Eric should use this time to think about how he can be a better student, and thus, a better practitioner and eventually, a good teacher. Mr. Malone explicitly said, "Teamwork makes the dream work." He was telling his staff exactly what to do in order to get his attention.

Up until this point, Eric has been exposed to several different cases of the ERs. He has been in close proximity to those who are infected, and as a result, he is now at risk of being a "carrier."

Eric dreaded entering the building on Monday morning. On the morning news, he saw a video clip of Cody Brooks being hounded on the street by the paparazzi. When Cody hit his breaking point, he turned around and bumped one of the cameras, sending it smashing to pieces on the ground. Of course, this caused a major ruckus with the paparazzi and created even more drama for Cody. There wasn't any word on whether Cody had been detained and questioned by the authorities, but the video of his rage had gone viral on various news outlets and social media.

Once in the office, Eric was surprised to see Cody Brooks, mere hours after the camera incident, perched against the doorway of Mr. Malone's office with Jack Sullivan at his side. Eric didn't want to stare, but he did, just long enough to take in Cody's appearance. As usual, Cody's relax-fit designer jeans were hanging low for the office environment. He wore branded sneakers, a simple button-down dress shirt with rolled-up sleeves, slightly revealing heavily tattooed arms, and an oversized baseball cap, which he quickly removed upon entering the office environment. Eric turned back to his computer to check the office

60

calendar. He was hoping that Theresa had posted something that would give him more insight into what caused Cody and Jack to show up without warning. Was Cody being dropped as a client? Was he headed to court for the camera incident? Before he could finish reading the morning's updates, he felt a tap on his shoulder. He looked up to see Theresa.

"Eric, Mr. Malone asks that you show Mr. Brooks to the men's room. Then show him around a bit."

With that request, she handed Eric a set of keys held together with a gold emblem. Everyone knew that the gold keys opened the door to the executive suite. Eric extended his hand to greet Cody. He couldn't wait to tell his buddies about this encounter later.

"Good morning, I'm Eric Woods."

Cody grabbed his hand and pulled him towards him, giving Eric one firm slap in the middle of his back.

"What up, my man?"

Eric led him down the hallway toward the restrooms, ignoring the curious eyes from his co-workers. He wondered why Mr. Malone had chosen him to escort such a high-stakes client. Cody figures his past experience as a student-athlete in college may have something to do with it, but he was not sure. He stood outside the door until Cody emerged from the men's room.

"Mr. Malone said you were interested in seeing the sales floor," Eric said.

"Whatever they say, man. They're just trying to get me out of that conference room while they debate about how to deal with the current dilemma I'm this time. It's cool, though. You got something to drink?"

Eric jingled the gold keys in his hand and led Cody toward the back of the office to an area that was rarely used except when Mr. Malone wanted a more relaxed atmosphere to discuss business with important clients. Eric unlocked the door and they stepped inside the lounge area. There was a bar area and a refrigerator with cold drinks. Cody grabbed the television remote and clicked it on. He found a sports channel and turned up the volume. Just as Eric handed Cody a sparkling water, the newscaster began reporting the details of the camera incident. Eric watched Cody's face.

"I don't even know why I turned this on," Cody said, turning down the volume in frustration. "They only report the side they want the public to see."

Eric handed Cody a glass of ice and said, "Well, that's journalism. They have to sensationalize the story to make people want to watch it."

Cody shook his head with irritation as he poured his drink.

"But this is not right. It's not what really happened."

They were both silent for a moment as they watched the footage of Cody's explosive encounter with the television on mute. It looked even worse with no audio. Eric chose his next words carefully.

"So, if that video was spun to twist public opinion, what really happened?"

Cody gulped his drink and rubbed his face with his palms as if the world was perched on his shoulders.

"I have no problem being filmed," he said. "They made that video look like I'm just some kind of spoiled athlete who doesn't want my picture taken. I'm cool being in the spotlight if they are cool, man."

"Yeah, I get that feeling about you from what I've seen on your social media pages," Eric said.

"Exactly! Man, I'm not one of those athletes who get famous, and then, all of a sudden acts too cool to be on camera. I know what I signed up for!"

"So, how did you end up breaking that guy's camera?" Eric asked.

Cody sighed, "I was out there with my little sister. She's only 17. Still in high school. I might have signed up for this life, but she didn't."

"Maybe they thought you were on a date. For a bachelor like you, that's juicy gossip for the tabloids."

Cody shook his head emphatically. "No, I don't believe that for a second. Anybody with half a brain can look at my little sister and see she's a kid. If they had just snapped a quick picture and kept it moving, I would have been fine. But they were hounding her, sticking the camera right in her face, yelling inappropriate questions at her. It was crazy."

"You're clearly passionate about your sister's safety. Where was your bodyguard?"

Cody buried his face in his hands for a moment. When he looked up, Eric could see regret in his eyes.

"I usually have him with me, but this *one* time, I decided to step out and grab dinner with my sister. I really didn't think that much drama could go down in *fifteen minutes*. It was like a circus. They kept shoving that camera in her face, she looked so scared, and...I just snapped and bumped the guy's camera getting out of there."

Eric grabbed a bottle of water for himself and moved to the other side of the bar where he hopped on a barstool.

"You have kind of blown up in popularity and fame, whether it's been good exposure or bad exposure. Once you give these reporters and photographers a piece of something interesting, they're like vultures—"

"I know, I know," Cody said, exasperated, "But I thought it would stay focused on me, not on her. She's innocent."

"It doesn't matter," Eric told him. "She's connected to you. That's all they need."

They sat in silence for a moment while Cody let Eric's words sink in.

"I don't know what to do at this point," Cody said finally.

Eric thought of his own experience and his days in college school as a rising athlete. He remembered losing his cool in one game, and after that, it always felt like everyone in the stands was waiting for him to blow up at every foul and every bad call. It was Eric's father who told him he had to counter the bad rep with good behavior to let people see his charitable side. That's how Eric got involved in his neighborhood community center and started working with troubled youth.

"You're going to have to put yourself out there as more than just a hothead athlete. Generate some positive press. Let them catch you doing some positive things for a change," he said.

Cody frowned, "You mean like, stage working for a charity or something? Go down to the soup kitchen and help out so that it can be on the 6 o'clock news?"

"Well, not exactly," Eric said. "It should be more genuine than that. Something you would do anyway even if the cameras were not involved. What do you care really about besides basketball?"

Cody cracked his knuckles as he sat deep in thought.

63

"I don't know. Besides keeping my little sister safe and helping to care for my mother, who has lupus, I don't really have time to think about much else."

Cody removed his baseball cap and slowly rubbed his temples with his fingertips. He didn't look like a twenty or twenty-two-year-old kid in this moment. Eric could see the stress, fatigue and worry in his posture and countenance.

"Maybe there's something you can do for the lupus community. There are so many people suffering from that illness."

"I can't save the world, man."

"It's not about saving the world," Eric said, "It's about doing something that shows what kind of person you really are. You say the media has you confused, right? Set them straight by being known for doing something good besides having a great post-game."

Cody nodded and reached out to give Eric another backslapping handshake.

"You really gave me some good perspective man. I appreciate it."

*Eric doesn't have all the answers. He's still trying to figure out his own place with ESE However, he has one thing his colleagues' lack - the ability to see the perspective of an up-and-coming young man who is teetering between boyhood and manhood, like himself. The guidance he is able to give Cody Brooks is from a place of personal experience.

It never occurred to Cody his antics could affect those close to him. Just like the symptoms of the ERs are contagious, Cody Brooks' celebrity status is just as infectious. His response to that role affects his sister, mother, the team, his community back home, agent, and the executives at Exponential. There are times when just being connected to a person can be a risk. In some cases, this could be detrimental to one's success. In other cases, such as the connection between Eric and Cody, this can lead to teachable moments.

As Eric and Cody parted ways, Eric promised him that he would help locate charities and non-profit organizations dedicated to research and support for those living with lupus like Cody's mother. Eric tried to ignore all the eyes on the two of them as they followed Theresa back toward Mr. Malone's office and shook hands again. It felt cool being the first one in the office to connect with the company's superstar client on a personal level. At the same time, the negative press was the driving factor behind everyone's interest.

Sure enough, Carl was waiting for him when he returned to his cubicle.

"I saw you hanging out with King Cody Brooks," he joked.

Eric smiled and shrugged, "I was just doing what Mr. Malone asked of me."

"Good for you. There's something brown on your nose."

Eric rolled his eyes. He had fallen for that joke several times already. Carl was always accusing someone of brown-nosing or sucking up to the boss.

"It's not like I had a choice, Carl. Come on, give me a break."

Carl hiked up his pants legs and sat on the edge of Eric's desk, not bothering to move the papers and files aside.

"I guess that makes sense," he said. "You're the help. They always get the help to do the dirty work."

"I wouldn't call it dirty work. It wasn't bad. There's more to him than meets the eye with Cody. I mean, he's not really like the image painted of him by the media. I guess you have to be a little more open-minded."

"Oh really? What does he do? Volunteer at the old folks' home and spend time with them?"

"No, Carl, but he definitely does care about more than cars and a good time. I think he's just misunderstood. Let's not forget he's around twenty-one years old and a human being. He's bound to make a mistake or two at his age."

"I understand his generation just fine. He doesn't want to work hard for anything. He wants everything handed to him on a silver platter. He chases a ball up and down the court. We're the ones doing all the hard work here. And what does he do? Show up to our office building with pants hanging down past his boxer shorts and we're supposed to smile and grin if we want to get paid."

Eric did not interrupt Carl's rant. He was becoming accustomed to these occasional gripe sessions that seemed to paralyze Carl with frustration. Carl literally could not move one foot in front of the other and make his way back to his own desk until he unleashed a barrage of complaints. It was true that Cody did not have to do much knowledge of the behind-the-scenes work it takes to position him as a brand at this point in his career. A large part of his job was purely to perform on the court. Cody's job is equally hard on the performance side, which Carl failed to acknowledge. The people who kept the wheels turning in his career probably work hard too, but don't receive the same level of accolades and compensation. But that was just the nature of the business. It amazed Eric how much Carl let it unravel him.

"Everybody has their own role to play, Carl," he said cautiously, not wanting to ruffle more feathers.

"Where did you get a response like that, kid?" he asked annoyed. "Did you just pop a quarter in a machine and get that clichéd phrase to shut me up?"

"No, Carl, I didn't mean—"

"Well, that's what it sounds like, like bubblegum. You basically pulled a general, bubblegum response from your Rolodex full of non-substantive, unoriginal catchphrases. And then, tried to pass it off to me as if it was something profound that could change my outlook. Don't insult me like that."

"Look, Carl, I didn't mean to…The last thing I want is to offend—"

"That's the problem with your generation," Carl interrupted again. "You and that kid with the words cut into his hair and pictures tattooed all over his arms - none of you guys are original. You're an apprentice! Your entire job is built around sponging. And that superstar athlete who somehow *enlightened* you today, he can't even handle his own affairs off the court. He's like a student who got suspended from school and we're like his parents, meeting with the principal to negotiate a second chance. Give me a break."

Eric watched in disbelief as Carl pumped a dollop of hand sanitizer into his palm and stormed off toward his own desk.

Carl Clinger is a fan of good old-fashioned hard work. There was once a time when success was attained primarily through hard work and sacrifice. People went to college if they wanted a professional career, and they put in many years of tenacity if they wanted the big bucks and

promotions. Cody Brooks' mishandling of h,
insult to someone like Carl Clinger who has w
the old-fashioned way and earned his strip
academics, hard work and perseverance.

The mistake Clingers like Carl often make is
personal views with the changing times. They are
methodologies that it angers them when new
alternate ways to accomplish the same thing. Carl i   ɔ ι0
how people conducted business when he first enterec   ɔ ιnat he is
too preoccupied to see that Cody Brooks can be an assɔι to his career.

- Are you able to spot when you have picked up ER-like symptoms
  from someone else?

- How can you lead others in positive directions by teaching them
  through your own experiences?

- What opportunities right in front of you could be going unnoticed
  because of your resistance to change?

Chapter 11
Ducking & Dodging

Over the next few days, Eric avoided irritating Carl any further by throwing himself into researching the entry-level executive position. Brenda wasn't much help these days, but he did take advantage of opportunities to watch Larry and Daria so he could get ideas on how to generate new business. He took his notes home so he could study in the evenings. It was difficult at work because every time Eric tried to capitalize on teachable moments, someone needed something filed, copied, stapled or delivered. The sudden interruptions sometimes got the best of Eric, but this was part of the learning curve he had to embrace in the transition from sports to the business world.

On one particular day, Larry dropped a mountain of random folders on his desk along with an electronic label maker machine.

"Hey, buddy, I need my filing system updated. This stuff is all out of order and it's driving me crazy. Organize this for me and color code it so that it makes sense."

"I'd love to help you, Larry, but I'm shadowing Daria today on a sales call."

Larry shrugged as if he did not understand the dilemma and nodded his head.

"Yeah, yeah…that's cool. You can do both. You're like a super apprentice, buddy."

With that, he walked away. Eric groaned aloud before he realized what he was doing. Brenda peeked over the side of the cubicle and pushed her glasses up onto her nose.

"See what I mean?" she hissed, her eyes darting back and forth like a spy.

Eric shot her an annoyed look "Not now, Brenda."

"Hey, don't shoot the messenger," Brenda whispered. "It's not like you can say I didn't warn you. Larry does *none* of his own deskwork. While the rest of us slave over files and spreadsheets all day, he's out socializing and calling it work. Humph."

"I don't think I'm really in a position to say no," Eric whispered back as he thumbed through Larry's towering heap of files.

"Well, being a 'yes' man is not getting you anywhere. You keep letting him push you around. He's going to become the bane of your existence. On top of that, he's getting away with murder! He's misusing company time and letting the brunt of the work fall on you. It's not right!"

As Brenda's words sunk in, Eric could feel the blood rushing to his face.

"I'm going to have to cancel shadowing Daria again."

Brenda shook her head in pity and her eyeglasses slipped back down the bridge of her nose. "I'm telling you, I think he's doing it on purpose."

Eric frowned and looked up from the files. "What would he gain from that?" he asked.

Brenda put her finger to her lips and looked around furtively for a moment.

"You never noticed how he comes with an armful of busywork when it's common knowledge that you are shadowing for the day? He's sabotaging you."

Eric shook his head no. "That doesn't make any sense. He's already an executive. I don't threaten his position at all. Why would he care whether or not I get the promotion?"

"Don't you get it?" Brenda asked in a forceful whisper. "Malone is going to take a few accounts from each of us and give them to the new executive. He has to inflate the new person's client list as a head start. You work pretty closely with Larry. You know a lot of inside information about his clients and his relationships with them. You could probably sweep a few, right from under his feet. He doesn't like anything that feels like a threat. If I were you, I'd shove that pile of garbage right back on his desk and go do something that actually matters to your career. Otherwise, you're going to be the 'Super Intern' forever."

With that, Brenda darted down back into the depths of her cubicle before Eric could refute her suggestion. Without pondering, Eric hopped out of his chair, scooped up the mound of Larry's paperwork, and made his way to Larry's cubicle where he dropped the files in the center of the desk. He thought about leaving a note to explain why, but decided that the unfiled work said enough. He checked his watch and headed to Daria's desk. Ironically, Daria was labeling her own files.

"I'm ready when you are," Eric said as he eyed Larry's desk, hoping to avoid a confrontation that would thwart his plans of leaving the office with Daria.

Daria looked up and nodded. "Great, let's head out." She stood up, grabbed her briefcase, and turned toward the elevators, which happened to be directly across from Larry's desk.

"Actually," Eric said, "Can we take the north side elevators? They're closer to the coffee shop in the lobby and I want to grab some caffeine to go."

Daria checked her watch, smiled, and said, "Sure, no problem. Let's go."

Eric looked over his shoulder one last time as they hurried toward the other side of the office.

Brenda Blamer is so contagious that she manages to change Eric's entire outlook on a situation. Yes, the mountain of administrative work Larry Leaper dumps on him annoys Eric, but he does not consider it to be a conspiracy until Brenda Blamer influences him. Whether Larry Leaper resents the opportunity Eric is facing, it does not change the fact that Eric is an apprentice. It is, in fact, Eric's job to complete administrative tasks whenever he's asked. Eric allows his emotions to cloud his thinking, loses sight of his work responsibilities, and makes a conscious decision to avoid Larry Leaper.

The avoidance method is a problem because it is passive-aggressive. Instead of making it clear where he stands, Eric creates a situation that is unclear and illusive. He even goes so far as to take a detour out of the office to avoid running into Larry Leaper. He pushes his deception a step further by misleading Daria Do-er with a false story. These are all amateur moves that make Eric look juvenile and unprofessional rather than ready to take on an executive position.

Remaining proactive can create decent and honest character. Eric can be proactive by simply telling Larry Leaper, "I will absolutely sort your files for you after I complete this sales call with Daria. You can expect those files on your desk by tomorrow morning." If Eric does not have time to fit the filing into his schedule, he can stay late at the office to display his dedication to the job. It will be a sacrifice, but many great things can and do come with sacrifice when you are trying to establish yourself in the business world.

- How can you thwart the damaging effects of catching one of the ERs from someone close to you?

- Where can you find moments of sacrifice for the sake of the bigger picture?

- When someone is taking advantage of you, how can you stand up for yourself without compromising your professional performance?

Chapter 12

Dust Yourself Off and Try Again

Daria's client was not amused by Cody Brooks' antics. Daria already knew this and tried to focus on the numbers. She'd done a great deal of research on the sales demographics of Arctic Freeze pain cream. Other well-known brands were making it difficult for Arctic Freeze to expand.

"Cody Brooks is one of today's most promising athletes," Daria exclaimed. "He has the perfect combination of natural skill and star power backed by a rags-to-riches story. His story resonates with the public, and he can generate the kind of buzz to help Arctic Freeze become the number one topical agent for the everyday American athlete or anyone with joint pain."

Eric was mesmerized by the fact that Daria wasn't just charismatic in her delivery but knowledgeable as well. Unfortunately, Daria's presentation did not seem to compel Mr. Slovik.

"When I think of Mr. Brooks," he began, "I think of his track record of negative press and assaults on paparazzi. I don't think of a wholesome, All-American athlete using a pain cream after games."

Eric had to agree. Mr. Slovik was right. Cody's decisions had damaged his image. Somehow, Daria appeared unfazed by the negative assessment.

"And you are not alone, Mr. Slovik. That is precisely why I am here. Your product can not only benefit from Mr. Brooks' celebrity influence, but it can also help him rebuild his tarnished public persona."

"I am not in the business of public relations," Mr. Slovik responded.

Daria's eyes were still gleaming with optimism. "I understand that wholeheartedly," she continued, "but in the past five years, your brand has lost several of its major retail distributors. It could only be a matter of time before your product line is made available exclusively via internet commerce. Mr. Brooks, however controversial his personal life, could be the person that helps make your product a household name."

Mr. Slovik's assistant entered with a DVD in her hand. Eric shifted uncomfortably in his seat as the she turned on the flat-screen television mounted at the front of the room. She loaded the DVD, and the four of them spent the next ten minutes watching a montage of all of Cody Brooks' bad press from various news outlets. It was embarrassing. Eric wanted the floor to open up and eat him alive. Mr. Slovik had done a great deal of homework on Cody, and he obviously did not like what he found.

"As you can see, Ms. Young, your client is not the type of celebrity power my company is interested in using to endorse our brand. Sure, he may boost sales for a month or two if we plaster his face on our product, but what about next year, or five years from now? I am thinking about the longevity of Arctic Freeze. In my opinion, Mr. Brooks and the word longevity do not belong in the same sentence at this time."

Daria smiled and nodded. "I understand your position, Mr. Slovik," she said, standing to her feet.

Mr. Slovik and his assistant stood also. Eric watched as Daria reached out to shake their hands.

"Hopefully, we can work together in some capacity in the future. Thank you for your time, and enjoy the rest of your day."

Eric gathered their documents and followed Daria out of the conference room. He had never seen someone take rejection so casually. When they were sitting in Daria's car in the parking garage he asked, "Weren't you supposed to offer rebuttals or negotiate the deal more?"

Daria turned the key in the ignition and pulled out of the parking space.

"Eric, you have to assess your clients before you even meet them. I already knew that there was a slim chance that Frances Slovik would be interested in an endorsement deal with Cody. Just as he did his homework on our client, I did *my* homework on Arctic Freeze. They are not a risk-taking company and they stick to a wholesome image. I knew what the odds were when I stepped into the room."

"Then why even waste your time?" Eric asked.

"You saw it as a waste of time?" Daria asked.

"Well...it just seems that you could have spent that time with a more surefire company. Carl once told me that a smart executive knows his client's history and business, and if it looks like the deal is impossible, it doesn't make sense to spend a lot of time trying to build a hypothetical portfolio for them."

Daria stopped at a red light and looked over at Eric thoughtfully.

"If I never approach prospective clients because I think they are going to be difficult, how will I know what is surefire and what isn't? I never view a prospective client as a waste of time. You never know when you might hear a 'yes' from the very person you assumed would say 'no.' I respect Carl as a veteran exec, but I have to disagree with his logic. Just having the meeting is enough to make a positive impression. Mr. Slovik isn't too keen on Cody Brooks, but now he has met me, Daria Young. He has my card. He's seen the way I present a deal. I've built a bridge."

"But you got shut down. You didn't get the endorsement," Eric said.

Daria chuckled, "Your idea of 'shut down' differs quite a bit from *my* idea of 'shut down.' Sometimes, you have to hear more than a few 'no's' before you get a 'yes,' Eric. I planted a seed of rapport with Mr. Slovik, and one day when I'm working with a client, who would be perfect for the Arctic Freeze image, I'll pay Mr. Slovik another visit. Even the 'no's' are opportunities."

Eric thought about Daria's words during the entire ride back to the office. He could not take his mind off the stack of work he'd shoved back onto Larry's desk in a moment of frustration. He could not help but think to himself how organizing the paperwork could have been equivalent to receiving a "no." Just because he did not particularly enjoy filing did not mean there wasn't value in completing it.

Daria is infected with a strong strain of being a Do-er. Fortunately for her, the symptoms of being a Do-er can do more good than bad when they multiply and spread. Daria handles rejection well. She respects the client's rebuttal, has an honest exchange of information, and leaves the door open for future opportunities. Being a Do-er does not guarantee success. What Daria mastered is how doing your homework, presenting your best effort, and respecting the opinions of others are all aspects of the process, which you can control. Daria has those aspects of the meeting under her control, and so she is able to walk away with confidence. She put in 100% even when the outcome is not what she desires.

- *How can you plant seeds of productivity in the face of what seems insurmountable?*

- *In the face of difficulty, what parts of the challenge are you able to control?*

- *When the door closes in your face, how can you ensure that it is simply closed but not locked?*

Chapter 13
Class Is in Session

Some people back at the office could not wait to question Daria and Eric about the outcome of the sales call. Mr. Slovik had quite a reputation. Daria knew her co-workers were only asking to reassure themselves they weren't the only ones struggling. There had been very little new business generated, and it was creating a heightened sense of anxiety around the office.

Making matters worse, that nasty bug was still going around and five more people called in sick the previous week. Brenda could be heard threatening that if she took the illness home and passed it to her baby, she was going to take an indefinite leave. Some people almost wished she would get sick already so there would be a bit of peace around the office without her incessant complaining. Carl mentioned a few times that no one ever let a little bug stop them from coming into the office and getting the job done. He liked to brag that he hadn't taken one sick day in the last 5 years, and he wasn't about to take one now.

Eric went straight to Larry's desk when he returned to the office and picked up the stack of paperwork he had been asked to sort earlier. He ignored Brenda's disapproving headshake as he headed back to his desk to work on the files. Watching Daria's cool demeanor had motivated him. He admired how Daria didn't get deflated one bit after Slovik rejected her proposal. Eric was an hour into printing labels and sticking them onto recycled folders when his desk phone rang. He answered, "Eric Woods."

"Hey...Eric, it's Cody."

Cody sounded nervous. Eric put his supplies down and looked around before responding, "Hey...everything okay?"

"Yeah...well, actually...I'm down in Lincoln Heights, and I lent my friend my ride, and now I can't get ahold of him. I would call Jack, but...he's pretty tired of dealing with all this, you know."

Lincoln Heights was one of the roughest neighborhoods in the city, and it was where Cody grew up.

"And I guess you can't exactly call a cab...you being Cody Brooks and all."

"Exactly...I really don't have anybody else who could pick me up right now. Everybody here in my crew has had too much to drink, and I don't feel good about them driving. I've been here all night and most of the morning, so if you could do this favor for me, it would get me out of a major jam. Besides, today is my off-day, and I really need to get home to rest up for my next road trip."

Eric sighed, hesitated, and then said, "Take down my cell phone number, and text me the address."

Driving down the streets of Lincoln Heights, Eric could not understand what would make a superstar like Cody Brooks want to return to such a neighborhood. Many of the buildings were rundown and full of graffiti, while broken bottles and trash littered the streets and sidewalks. As Eric was driving, he realized regardless of what he thought, Cody still considered this home. He slowed down in front of the address Cody sent to him. Eric did not want to get out of the car, so he beeped the horn. No one came outside. Hesitantly, he stepped outside, locked his car doors, and headed through a rickety chain-link gate and up to the front door of the house. He could hear loud music blasting front inside, practically shaking the windows of the house. After banging on the door three times, it swung open. A huge guy dressed in a ripped tank top stood on the other side holding a bottle in his hand.

"What?" He asked, clearly annoyed.

"Hey, I'm Eric. I'm looking for Cody."

The guy motioned with his head for Eric to step inside. Eric glanced inside the home and hesitated before shaking his head, thinking it was best to stay outside.

"Can you just tell him that I'm outside waiting for him?" he asked.

"Yeah, I'll get him," the big guy told Eric before turning back inside.

A few minutes later, Cody emerged, and the two of them jumped into Eric's car.

"Thanks so much, man. I appreciate it. I hope I didn't get you in trouble at the firm for coming down here."

Eric shook his head. "I took a half day. There's some virus going around the office, so when people say they need to head out, nobody really asks questions anymore."

"Okay, good. I didn't want that Malone guy you work for to rip your head off. I just couldn't think of anybody else who would be cool enough to scoop me up and not want something in return, if you know what I mean. Plus, I got a lot drama going on in life and I need to keep things on the low."

Eric stopped at a red light and looked over at Cody who was wearing a lot bling around his neck, wrists and in his ears.

"So, this friend of yours just took your car? I mean, did you report it stolen?"

Cody frowned, "Nah...he'll bring it back. He's just showing off with my whip, and he'll return soon. He'll call me later tonight."

Eric couldn't believe his ears. "Cody, it's a car...not a favorite shirt or a cell phone."

"I'm telling you...he'll bring it back. I've known this guy since we were kids."

"Even more reason this doesn't make sense," Eric said. "If he's your friend, he wouldn't have left you stranded."

Cody shrugged and scooted the seat back. "You just don't get it, E. This is my family. These are the people I grew up with before the league. I trust them. That house you were just in...I used to go there and eat dinner with my friend's family. There were times they'd spend their last few dollars on me so I would have what I needed to play ball. I'm not gonna report my car stolen and get my boy in trouble when I know he's just cruising in a car he could only dream of owning."

Eric didn't respond. He turned down the next street. When the light turned green, he looked around at the dilapidated housing.

"I'm not judging you or your friend, Cody. But you might have to think twice about visiting your old neighborhood as often for the sake of your career right now."

Cody shook his head like Eric just didn't understand. "You sound like my agent. Jack wants me to hang out with these celebrity guys and go to upscale places. But this is where I'm from, and I don't want to forget it. I don't want to be that guy who makes it big and acts like he's better than the people he left behind."

"That's not what I am suggesting," Eric said, "but you are Cody Brooks. You are a high-profile public figure whether you want to accept it or not. You are a multi-millionaire. Everybody from your 'hood' does not get to experience things on the same level just because they grew up with you. I saw activity in that house that could cripple your career. Since they are your friends, you might have to help them learn how to support you in protecting your career. I'm just saying, be smart about it. The opportunity you have right now is not going to last forever. Take full advantage of it."

For once, Cody did not have a response.

"There comes a point when you have to love people from afar. I can tell you really want to show your friends that you haven't changed, that you still care about them. You can still help them, but don't hurt yourself in the process."

Eric looked over at Cody and noticed his eyes were watery, but he looked away quickly as to not embarrass him. Neither of them said anything for a while. Finally, as they reached Cody's exit on the interstate, he began directing Eric toward his house. It was really more like a mansion. Eric punched in the numbers to the gate and eased his car up the winding driveway. As beautiful and majestic as the house looked, Eric couldn't help but notice it did not look like Cody even lived there. All of plants out front were dead and there were packages stacked to the doorknob.

"So, what are you going to do now?" he asked Cody who didn't seem to want to get out of the car.

"Play video games…maybe go downstairs to the gym and work on my jump shot."

Eric nodded and waited. Cody wasn't making a move to get out of the car, and it seemed like he wanted to say something.

"Everything okay?" Eric asked finally.

"Do you ever feel like it's only a matter of time before you mess things up? Like, what's the point because it's all going to come crashing down anyway?"

Eric frowned. Cody sounded eerily similar to Carl who often did not return sales calls because he felt like they would amount to nothing but a pile of unwanted paperwork.

"Cody, you can't think like that. If you look at an opportunity as futile just because the odds are stacked against you, then you have lost before you even gave it a chance. So what if things don't work out perfectly?"

"If it doesn't work out, then all the hard work, sweat and tears were for nothing," Cody said.

"That's not true," Eric replied. "You would at least gain lessons and learn from the experience. Let's be real...you might get traded next year. You could break your leg. Then again...you might not. You could end up being one of the greatest players that ever played the game. How will you know unless you put yourself out there?"

"It's just a lot of pressure," he muttered.

"Pressure is good," Eric said, playfully nudging Cody's shoulder. "Good pressure can show you what you're made of. If it helps, my mom once told me, if you know how to harness pressure, you can make beautiful diamonds from a lump of coal. So, feeling pressure can't be all bad. It pushes you to your limit. Forget about all the people waiting for you to fall. Think about all the people rooting for you to succeed. I think they'd be more disappointed if you give up to go back to just hanging out in the 'hood' with your boys. You owe it to yourself and all of the people who have supported you to give it everything you've got."

Having spent time with Daria, Eric seems to be displaying symptoms of being a Do-Er. He is forward thinking and sharing the wealth of knowledge in a critical moment. Eric is able to be that voice of reason to keep Cody Brooks grounded, not as a basketball star but as a young man who is having a difficult time making the right choices right now. Eric just learned a lesson about embracing experience and accepting letdowns as opportunities to improve. Now he is able to pass on the lesson to someone else. It is what makes a Do-er unique from the other ERs. It's the most teachable position.

As a result, Eric is better at fighting off the symptoms of the other ERs. When he returns to the office, Eric chooses to ignore Brenda Blamer's opinion and does what he considers to be the right thing. That's a valuable lesson for anyone who works with many different personalities. Eric finds a way to work with Brenda Blamer without necessarily sharing her sentiment. Also, when Cody Brooks decides to "cling" to his past life by pondering whether his old low-pressure life is better than his celebrity, Eric blocks the Clinger affliction like a seasoned pro! Clinging to easier, painless and low-risk situations is not a way to succeed in life. Daria Doer showed Eric this during the sales call with Arctic Freeze and Eric is able to pass on that philosophy to Cody.

- *How can you "rub off" on others who appear to be infected with Blamer, Clinger or Leaper ways of thinking?*

- *How can you be a teacher or even an example to someone who may be more impressionable, and therefore more susceptible to the ERs?*

- *When you stumble over hurdles, how can you show someone else the lesson to be learned in the obstacle?*

Chapter 14
"And the Grand Prize Goes to..."

A few weeks later, Mr. Malone made a decision concerning the promotions. He had watched each of his executives and monitored their business dealings. Everyone met in the conference room, accepting a couple squirts of hand sanitizer from an automatic dispenser on their way in the door. Eric looked around the table at the executives he had assisted for many months. Brenda pushed her glasses onto her nose and sighed in annoyance. Larry tapped his fingers atop the table impatiently and looked at his watch. Carl was expressionless; in fact, it looked like he was nodding off a bit. Daria sat quietly with a tablet in front of her, ready to take notes if needed. Eric checked out the other apprentices as well. They looked just as nervous as he felt.

"We have seen quite a bit of action this quarter," Mr. Malone began in his signature booming voice.

"The thing that makes a great salesperson is not just the amount of money he or she generates for the company. It is a combination of revenue, courage, accountability, excellence, and innovation. Although I acknowledge that we have several high-performing executives here at Exponential, I can honestly say together, you are much stronger and much more effective."

He looked around the room for a moment and smiled, letting his teamwork philosophy settle in the minds of his audience.

"However," Mr. Malone continued, "there comes a time when one of the group members must take on greater challenges and step into the shoes of leadership. I need a sales manager who is going to go the extra mile for this company. This person needs to have the insight to fit together the puzzle pieces of our staff. That person is..."

Eric had an urge to produce the sound of a drumroll with his fists on the table. The suspense was killing him.

"Daria Young."

A few shocked gasps could be heard around the table. Daria was a newer executive, someone with only a few years of experience that paled in comparison to more veteran executives like Carl. Finally, someone started applauding and everyone else slowly joined in. Eric took that moment to glance around at the stunned faces of some of his executives. Carl looked sick to his stomach. Larry's jaw twitched in anger. Brenda stared at the table, no doubt entertaining the conspiracy theories in her head.

When everyone finished congratulating Daria, Mr. Malone moved on to the other announcement; he had to choose an apprentice to promote into Daria's now vacant former position.

"Part of my decision to promote an apprentice was, of course, to do my hiring in-house," Mr. Malone began. "Why go outside to find a replacement when I have brought on some of the most amazing apprentice salespeople already?"

Eric felt someone pat him on his back encouragingly but didn't turn to look. The anticipation was killing him.

"Without further ado, I would like to announce that our newest junior account executive is…"

Eric secretly crossed his fingers at his side where no one could see.

"Chloe Sanders."

Eric exhaled slowly when he did not hear his name. He felt a pang in his chest but smiled anyway and began clapping along with his coworkers. Chloe, the redhead whom he dumped on a couple of times, grinned from ear to ear and stood to shake Mr. Malone's hand. Deep down, Eric knew she deserved it. She came in early and stayed late each day. She never complained, not even once. She studied the books and the spreadsheets with attention to detail that had more to do with genuine interest than ambition. She was the perfect choice for promotion.

Everyone filed out of the conference room and headed toward their respective cubicles. Eric stopped by Carl's desk to ask if he needed help with a portfolio he was building for Audio Flex. When he got there, he found Carl stacking and arranging files that didn't really need to be fixed on his desk.

"Everything okay?" Eric asked with trepidation.

Carl shot him a look as if he was being ridiculous.

"Come on, kid. You think I really care about that little promotion? I make more money than that position already with all the years I've been here. I'm fine as an account executive. I've made a decent living out of it, and I know exactly what I'm doing each day. There's no guessing."

Eric frowned, "But…you didn't want it at *all?*" he asked.

Carl shrugged, "I really don't care. I'm comfortable with my client list. I've built relationships with my clients. I don't have to study reports all night or extinguish fires. I don't have to manage anything but my money and myself. Besides, why would I want to take on more work?"

Eric was dumbfounded. It occurred to him that Carl literally had no ambition to move his career forward. His lackadaisical attitude and bare minimum contentment actually made Eric feel sorry for him.

Before he left for lunch, Eric stopped by Larry's cubicle as well. The office had been pretty quiet throughout the day as the dust settled from the morning's promotions. Eric wanted to pop in and give a word of encouragement to each executive with whom he had worked.

"How's it going?" he asked as he approached Larry's desk.

Larry had a spread of vending machine junk food laid across his desk. He was snacking on a combination of chocolate chip cookies and nacho chips. Eric cringed as Larry stuffed a bit of both into his mouth.

"It's going all the way to the top!" Larry exclaimed in a strange, overly excited voice. He flipped through his files so quickly that Eric wondered if he was even reading them.

"You need me to find something for you?" Eric offered, frowning at the way Larry threw the top file folder aside and began destroying the organization of the second one.

"No, buddy, I got it. I'm trying to find the projections for Arctic Freeze."

"I filed it in the other drawer under 'forecasts,'" Eric said.

Larry nodded and put his finger in the air as if a light bulb turned on inside his head.

"Anyway, I just wanted to pop in and see if you needed my help or if—"

"Look," Larry interrupted him, "you can cut the concerned, proactive intern act. You don't have to impress me anymore, buddy. I'm on my way out."

"On your way out?"

Larry nodded, "Yeah. I accepted a position with Media Star Marketing. I start immediately."

"This is not because of today's announcement, is it?"

Larry shrugged, "My time here is up Kid. It's happening because I'm not going to insult myself by sitting around waiting for management to acknowledge my worth. I am a dealmaker! I have countless firms to choose from. I don't have to sit here and watch rookies get promoted over me, while I never get recognized for helping to make this place successful. Sometimes you just have to know when to get off the bus."

"So, you're just going to *leave?*" Eric asked, "What about your clients? What about the business you generated here? I don't understand."

"You will one day," Larry said before releasing a loud, obnoxious belch.

"I just think you could benefit from continuing to work on what you already built."

Larry chuckled like what Eric said was the dumbest thing he ever heard.

"You can only build so much onto the same frame. Time to move on. I have a couple of buddies who advanced at Media Star within their first year. I need that kind of mobility. If you're smart, you'll realize you got a raw deal too. You deserved that spot today, buddy, not the redhead."

Eric realized there was nothing he could say to change Larry's outlook. It was a lost cause. He didn't want to stand there any longer to hear gibberish about why Chloe shouldn't have been chosen. He finally realized the more he listened, the more he might start to buy into it.

"Well, good luck to you, Larry. I hope you make it all the way to CEO."

Larry shook his hand quickly and turned back to combing through his files. No doubt, he was looking for information he could take with him to have an advantage over the people at Media Star.

Brenda was the last person Eric wanted to see after the morning's meeting. He already knew she was fuming at her cubicle, telling anyone she could how she was wronged. Eric wasn't sure if he had the patience to deal with Brenda at that particular moment. However, he was beginning to learn everyone could use a boost of positive reinforcement.

Brenda was sitting at her desk, staring at a data report in unusual silence. Eric couldn't remember ever seeing her so quiet.

"Everything okay over here?" he asked, leaning against the cubicle wall.

Brenda didn't look up from her computer. She wasn't wearing her glasses. She only took them off when she was stressed.

"You know, hard work does not get rewarded around here."

"I think Daria works *very* hard," Eric said, "I shadowed her for months, and she was pretty amazing."

"Eric, you see how much stuff I have on my desk. I think I've handled it pretty well over the years. It's like I get all the pointless busywork, and it's so much of it that it's almost impossible to get it done."

Eric sighed and did not respond. He finally could see that there was no use in pointing out Brenda's tardiness, how she used her time unwisely, her lack of organizational skills, or her tendency to gossip. Brenda was content to place blame on everyone except herself.

"Daria has easy accounts, and I know Malone fed her those leads," Brenda went on. "I know she got help from management. She got some great accounts this year. Of course she was going to shine with that type of clientele."

"Maybe you should focus on what's on *your* desk," Eric said quietly.

What he wanted to say was, *Even if you had those big, impressive clients like Daria, would you have managed them properly? Would you have shown up to their meetings on time? Would you have gone above and beyond for them?* But Eric knew that asking her these questions would be futile because she had all of her fingers pointed everywhere but at herself.

"I don't understand why you're over here trying to justify things that are just unfair. I don't get this diplomatic role you're playing, Eric. You should be just as angry. They gave the executive promotion to that girl! Aren't you angry?"

Eric frowned, "Why would I be angry?"

Brenda sighed, as if she didn't have the patience to sp him.

"What makes her better than you? You come in here and w as hard, if not harder than her, you have—"

"Let me stop you right there," Eric interrupted, straining to keep h voice even. "What you're saying isn't true. I can see areas where I could have been better, where I could have worked harder, areas where Chloe shined, where she wanted it more than me. So, no...I can't say that I'm angry. I think management made the right choice. And even if they didn't, what is complaining about it going to get me? What will that accomplish?"

"I'm not complaining," Brenda said, "I'm just stating the obvious. I'm laying out the facts."

"Those are not facts, Brenda. They're opinions. And at the end of the day, my opinion is not the deciding factor in the decisions my superiors make. I can protest or I can work harder and try again. I'm going to choose to do the latter."

Brenda sucked her teeth and waved Eric away dismissively.

"Let me know if you need my help with anything," Eric said. "I'm here to help you."   With those last words, he walked away and headed back to his desk.

Before he left for the day, Theresa stopped by Eric's desk with a message. "Mr. Malone wants to see you."

What could this be about? Eric followed her to the executive offices and stepped inside the door. He watched as Theresa exited and closed the door, leaving him alone in the room with Mr. Malone.

"Eric, have a seat. I called you in here because I overheard the conversation you had with Brenda Baker earlier today."

Eric's eyes widened for a second. If he was being fired, he wanted to kick himself for letting a silly conversation with Brenda jeopardize his own job.

"I hope I did not offend anyone," Eric said in a quiet voice.

"Not at all. I wanted to commend you."

"*Commend* me?"

"I would like you to know that you were considered for the junior executive position. Ms. Sanders was my ultimate choice because she had the tenacity I was looking for. However, my eye is on you as well. I have ɔu juggled assisting so many different personalities

ɑl months. I was impressed by your work and the

with our client, Cody Brooks and the positive effect

the business. Your professionalism, accountability

ɑre qualities I need on my team. So...with that

cannot offer you a promotion today, I want to

ᴜ continue doing what you are doing, and in the near

., ᵢ can see great opportunities opening up for you here."

Mr. Malone stood. Eric stood as well.

"Thank you so much, sir. Hearing you say that means a lot to me."

Mr. Malone held out his hand, and Eric accepted the firm handshake of solidarity.

Chapter 15

Vaccinate Yourself

The four ERs have been introduced. Which one are you? It's quite conceivable to think the ERs could be present in all of our personal, professional and social circles. Examining them to see which show up in your life personally is not meant to expose your shortcomings, but to merely help you identify areas that may need your attention. Eric's colleagues were so concerned with the "bug" going around, they were using hand sanitizer like there was a never-ending supply of it. Everyone's paranoia about getting sick was limited to the physical threat floating around the office. No one took notice of threats to their character, behavior or environment. No one noticed there was something far more contagious that went way beyond a cold or flu. It went far beyond a cough or sneeze. Just being in the same room with someone afflicted by the ERs exposed everyone to traits and characteristics that affected their work ethic, disposition, attitude, camaraderie and personal successes in the workplace. Think about more than just which precautions you should take to avoid catching something that could bring physical harm. What about things that could destroy your integrity, reputation, responsibility and ability to achieve a goal? How do you protect yourself from them?

There are ways around contracting all the ERs. Just like with any illness, it is imperative to take preventative measures against becoming "sick" as it relates to your behavior. Just like one avoids catching the common cold by limiting hand-to-hand contact, you can prevent catching the negative ERs by limiting your exposure to those already infected with this "behavioral virus."

Blamer Prevention

When the person in the next cubicle is complaining about their job by making excuses or pointing the finger at others when something goes wrong, make a concerted effort to avoid this person's behavior. Try to avoid giving this person the time to begin an explanation full of excuses and complaints. Simply tell him or her that you have more pressing matters to deal with elsewhere. After all, it only takes getting cut short so many times before a person realizes that no one is listening!

Often, when a person is a Blamer, the moans and grumbles are just a ploy for support or attention. So, give this person positive reinforcement. It is very important, however, to not encourage a Blamer to continue on this negative, self-destructive path. Don't even bother to question a Blamer about his or her paranoid grumbles; help them find a way out of a conversation clearly headed in a negative direction. Sometimes you may have to quarantine yourself from a person who is too far along in his or her affliction. Do not feel guilty. Some people are just too stubborn to make changes, even if examples are set for them. In this case, abandon all treatment and excommunicate yourself from interacting with the person. They are a risk to your well-being.

Sometimes when people gripe, it's because they simply feel misunderstood. They are trying to explain or rationalize their point of view, but fail to effectively articulate it. It comes out as complaining or blaming. Find out how you can help this person. There were countless opportunities for Eric to offer assistance to Brenda Blamer. Instead, he often took a backseat on the issue, assuming if he did not agree or disagree, he could stay in a neutral position. Once he realized Brenda Blamer's habit, he watched as her complaints spiraled into a whirlwind of negative energy. If you stop this person and ask how you can help, it may encourage them to transfer their focus from the problem to a solution.

The reason being a Blamer is so infectious is because it's a transfer of emotions. Transferring negative emotions from person to person is the worst way of being infected by the ERs. After all, you may never realize that you were exposed. A Blamer easily believes everything that does not go well for them is someone else's fault. This constant focus on others causes resentment and bitterness. A Blamer drags this animosity around and attempts to dump it on others by griping.

Have you ever had a conversation with someone who was unhappy about something, and by the end of the conversation, a weight has been lifted off this person's shoulders and placed upon your own? This is a classic case of "dumping." Do not allow Blamers to dump or transfer their stress, tension, anger and paranoia onto you. Shield yourself by spotting these intentions early and remain positive.

Clinger Prevention

When a colleague or co-worker refers to the "good ole' days" more than the average person, tread lightly around him or her. This person is living in the past. Do not get pulled into a retroactive time warp with someone who is simply fearful of failure. That's usually the backstory of a Clinger - a person who cannot bear the thought of rejection, and as a result, avoids opportunities altogether. How can that type of person lead anyone to success? How can that person be your guide if he or she is not moving forward during critical times in his or her own life? Being led by a Clinger is like walking in a perpetual circle.

One of the worst things to do when dealing with a Clinger is to adopt their philosophy, especially if you are seeking upward mobility. Clingers tend to offer a lot of information, usually wrought with recounting and reminiscing on past experiences. Because they tend talk a lot, it is easy to get pulled into the quicksand of Clinger mentality. The danger of this is it can be paralyzing. For instance, a Clinger may think your interest in a particular career move or new field is the wrong move. Whatever the reason for the Clinger's discouragement, this person is speaking failure into existence! Being around this person could cause you to doubt yourself and second-guess your decision.

Don't get comfortable around Clingers. Comfort and security are breeding grounds for Clinger infection. Clingers convince themselves that they should be thankful for what they have and circumstances "could be worse." They don't aspire to do more because they do not believe things can get better.

Have you ever witnessed a new hire at a corporation ascend the ladder so fast it made your head spin? The people left in the dust by management, unable to rise to greater positions, are typically the ones who do not think outside the box. In the eyes of their superiors, these people have been performing their jobs the same way for countless years and do not show any intentions of adjusting or adding to their methodologies. New hires usually come with new ideas. Promotions are offered to those who offer fresh, innovative ways of approaching the task at hand. To prevent becoming a Clinger, do not allow yourself to become comfortable with what you already know and do. Challenge yourself to surpass what is expected.

The ultimate challenge of a Clinger is to break out of the old school mentality, and leave past negative issues in the past. A good friend, Dr.

William Parham, a professor at Loyola Marymount College, uses the analogy of driving a car when discussing how people hold onto the past. It further elaborates on how to let go of a Clinger mentality. When driving, constantly looking in the rearview mirror is not needed to go forward. Just an occasional look will suffice. In fact, the front windshield of a car is large enough to stay mindful of oncoming traffic in order to avoid collisions on your way to your destination. Looking back is important, but if you are looking back throughout the entire journey, it will only be a matter of time before you crash. Your biggest question then will be, *how bad is the damage?* At a minimum, your car will be damaged, the other car will be damaged, and property may be destroyed. In an extreme situation, people could be badly hurt or even die. Looking in the rearview mirror can be costly. One must remember to keep in mind the past is not irrelevant, but the extent of importance is primarily based on personal decision.

Clingers make a special effort to point to out times when things were great for them or they were at their best. Unfortunately, unlike time, they stay trapped in that period and stop growing. They often try to get others to believe the particular period of time they are referring to was the greatest ever by asking others to endorse what they are saying. Often times, what Clingers say is ignored, and they are left to champion their own agenda.

They are often left to rant on by themselves because people are not buying what they are trying to sell. It is a self-serving mentality and it only *their* agenda. Clingers have to progress with the times or get left behind. This is often the case because they are unwilling to let go of the past and move forward.

This is not to say that the past is irrelevant; it is most relevant and best used for recognizing lessons learned and milestones earned.

Leaper Prevention

Leaping is not as much a sign of moving forward as much as it's a sign of possibly being out of control. Imagine driving on a roadway, crossing intersections and lanes, and ignoring one-way and U-turn signs. It's haphazard! Think about the areas of your life that always seem to be rushed. Are conversations with loved ones hurried? Do you finish the sentences of others to hurry the discussion along? If a parent, are the children rushed from place to place, whether it is to extra-curricular activities or to bed at the end of the night? Do you take the time to stop and breathe in between, just to connect with your family or casually converse? Typically, people who rush through everyday tasks also rush in other aspects of life, like careers and relationships.

Larry Leaper did not realize all of the rushing around, impatient behavior, and leaping from company to company, may not have been helpful to his overall advancement. He moved to a linear position that appeared more promising every other year. However, he spent a great deal of time moving side-to-side, not upward. It's like being cut and traded to a new professional sports team each year, just to have to start all over again. Even though a person may move to another team with a new coach and fresh possibilities, it takes time to adjust, learn a new system and develop team chemistry. Leaping from place to place, being the perpetual "new guy" can inhibit your ability to build professional bridges and solid business networks. Being upward bound is achieved through putting in a concerted amount of time and effort. Most importantly, it is fueled by dependability. It is important to avoid establishing a reputation of being the person who abandons ship every time something does not go your way. Employers may consider you to be high-risk, which could ultimately destroy confidence in your ability to exercise allegiance.

A Leaper appears eager on the surface. However, in most cases, they do not want to be boss; they just want to be relevant. A Leaper seeks acknowledgement. They pursue projects that lead to recognition. The progressive, pushy presence of the Leaper is really code for: "*I want to feel significant.*" Leapers are often the first to express dissatisfaction with leadership in the workplace. This is usually because they feel underappreciated and want to be included. Helping a Leaper feel rewarded at the beginning of his or her employment can help maximize productivity levels and eventually stimulate the entire work environment as well. It is important to *direct* a Leaper's energy and *encourage* their strengths. If recognition in the workplace is not found, Leapers will leave and continue to move from organization to organization.

The main way to build resistance against becoming a Leaper is to develop a great deal of patience for the process. Nothing grand happens overnight. No one is suggesting you accept circumstances, which may not be totally fulfilling. However, keep in mind that leaping blindly could have dire consequences. Learn to recognize the feeling of restlessness.

Become apt at determining whether it is just typical boredom or whether your situation has truly run its course. Once you decipher the root of your restlessness, strategize the best way to transition into the next phase of your life or career. The road to any goal worth reaching requires patience. It is the most effective preventative measure to avoid becoming a Leaper.

Next, approach one big task at a time. There are some people who develop many business ideas and try to pursue them all at once. A Leaper's strategy for accomplishing a goal is to cultivate eight good ideas, in order for maybe one or two to harvest. It is backwards thinking for you to split your time and energy eight ways; that strategy results in each task getting only 1/8 of your best. Avoid being a Leaper by writing a list of avenues to pursue, and cross them off *one-by-one* as you successfully execute them.

Lastly, avoid being a Leaper by knowing your role. When part of a team, be a team player. Don't try to wear the captain's hat, when you're not the captain. If you are the student, don't act like the teacher. If you are a rookie, take mental notes to improve your game every second on the bench. No matter how high one ascends up the ladder of corporate hierarchy, he or she may have to fill different roles on any given day. Remember, the path of a Leaper is a short road. A Leaper is not pausing to learn lessons along the way, so there are no yellow or red lights. A Leaper does not slow down or stop often enough to learn and appreciate what happens on the journey to the top. Unfortunately, when a person does not have traffic lights or signs guiding their route, the odds of a taking a wrong detour, having a collision or experiencing some type of destruction are much higher. This is the danger of being a Leaper. They move with the destination in mind, never stopping long enough to enjoy the breaks.

To avoid these pitfalls, document lessons learned along the way. What are you learning throughout the journey to success? How are you growing? Your answers to these questions will reveal the amount of growth in your quest. Reflect on accomplishments by pondering how you can advance them further and how you can assist someone else on a similar path. Reflect on your failures by contemplating how you can pick yourself up and begin on the road to redemption. When challenges occur, don't just abandon the team. Personally redeem yourself and learn from the process of falling, improving, and rebuilding for the betterment of the team. Learn enough from your journey to pass the knowledge and wisdom on to someone else.

Another very important factor to avoid being a Leaper is to find guidance in the most unlikely places. Larry Leaper was always too busy gazing up at the top of the mountain to stop and listen to those around him. Sometimes the greatest ideas come from the most unsuspecting sources. He did not see the value in learning from someone on his level and definitely not someone considered his subordinate. To combat this, acknowledge the value of everyone and find ways to fit into a team. How can you help others who can also help you? How can the group work for the greater good of the infrastructure as well as for each individual? Answer these questions wisely and implement them strategically for future success.

Do-er Creation

Recognize the symptoms of the three previous ERs. If exposure and infection have already occurred, do not waste time! Immediately treat the problem before it escalates into an epidemic that infects everyone in close proximity.

Here are some tips:
1. Recognize when others have "caught" one of the three negative ERs. Become knowledgeable about the symptoms a person displays when they are infected (e.g. complaining, blaming, leaving tasks undone or quitting them altogether, shoving work off onto others, etc.)
2. Prevent "catching" the ERs by building a positive attitude and work ethic on a daily basis. If needed, self-affirm throughout the day to stay positive. Do this as immunization against infection. Find a good mentor who understands how to help you find your way to the next level incrementally.
3. When you encounter a person who has "caught" one of the ERs, offer information on "treatments" to encourage improvement. Explain how they can be more accountable, focus on the task at hand, and remain more positive.

Truthfully, most of us have been afflicted with *each* of the ERs; either in our professional lives or even in our personal lives. These afflictions are curable. The first step is to acknowledge infection has taken place, and quite probably, may be highly contagious. Think about how many times you have said things similar to the characters in this book. We utter these comments about who's to blame, who doesn't have what it takes, and who stepped on whose toes without even realizing it. Imagine how many people have heard you say these comments, in passing or around the coffee machine. Unknowingly, you may have spread a symptom to someone else who just happened to be within earshot. This is how the ERs are spread from person to person.

It is essential to attack the symptoms of the negative ERs from the source. What is the source of your being a Blamer, Clinger or Leaper? Are you a Blamer because you refuse to let go of an incident with a past employer? Has fear of moving forward planted a Clinger mentality in you? When promotions are repeatedly passed to unqualified co-workers over you, does the Leaper appear? What personal triggers evoke symptoms? Don't simply treat the surface or the behavior itself; treat the cause or root of it all. Impatience, jealousy, pride, and insecurity are excellent springboards for the negative ERs. Don't try and fake treatment just to get the promotion; make real changes that apply to all areas and facets of your life.

Just like how one tries to stay hydrated throughout the day in order to heal from a common cold or flu, it is important for you to constantly feed on positive thoughts to combat the ERs. Even on your worst days, when it seems the odds are not stacked favorably, find something daily to celebrate. Affirm your success by taking the time to acknowledge your contributions, both large and small. You may not nail the big account, but you may satisfy a different client who shows their appreciation in a way that is worth much more than monetary value. Even if you are not the recipient of a big promotion, don't discount improvement in an area of your current position. "Revive your drive" by finding small ways to feel achievement throughout each day, even if it is simply completing and crossing each task off a daily "to-do" list.

Eric was not chosen for a promotion. Still, he did not view himself as having failed. It was a journey. The way he handled it was evidence his mind and heart were in the right place, and he was completely cured from the ERs. Unlike Brenda, Eric did not blame anyone else for his circumstances. He did not blame Chloe for being management's final choice. Instead, Eric was accountable, seeing exactly where he could enhance his performance. He did not decide to "jump ship" and leap to another company, like Larry Leaper, throwing a temper tantrum by packing up his desk and resigning. Instead, he remained loyal to the company and is enjoying the transition. He decided to remain in his current position, believing he had more to learn as an apprentice. Lastly, Eric did not simply shrug his shoulders and say, "Oh well" like Carl Clinger who was relieved to not take on extra duties. Instead, he planned to make positive changes in order to garner better results in the future. The only one of the ERs he decided to hold onto was being a Do-er. Daria Do-er knew how to grab opportunities in a way that was gracious, professional and rooted in integrity.

Here is the message: success is not guaranteed, even if you avoid catching the ERs or manage to cure yourself of the affliction. Achievement is not definite. What *is* definite is a stronger understanding of how actions and words can be contagious *and* affect character.

This tale of the "ERs" personifies which characteristics work together to develop a Do-er on the path to success in all facets of life. A Doer must have CONFIDENCE to make moves and changes without the fear of obstacles. A Do-er must possess the HUMILITY to learn from others. Regardless of his or her stature in life, knowledge of lessons learned along the way can have infinite value on that climb to the top. This individual has to encompass the right ATTITUDE. Many times, one's approach can be the deciding factor in the extent of successful results. A Do-er must display MENTAL TOUGHNESS in the face of adversity. There will be pitfalls in any journey. The tenacity and perseverance one maintains through failure fuels the fire in order to stay driven. A Do-er has to exhibit a great deal of PASSION. If one is invested in more than the dollar signs and fame, then possessing a directed source of enjoyment can make the turbulent climb worth so much more. This person must have the INGENUITY to reinvent him- or herself. Sometimes the roadmap has to be redrawn. Changes and modifications have to be made to reach the peak, and the detours can be enlightening. A Do-er should have the OPPORTUNISM to see hidden gems. There are often valuable tools, people and knowledge that already exist which are ripe to become opportunities. An optimistic outlook is almost always dependent on staying positive. Therefore, the Do-er must NEUTRALIZE NEGATIVITY. It can be difficult, but everyone can't be along for the ride. A Do-er must be skillful in determining when to remove negative elements, including people, from his or her journey in order to have a true chance at reaching the ultimate goal. Lastly, a Do-er must possess an inner voice that is rooted in SPIRITUAL SYNERGY. Do-ers trust and transition beyond what the eye can see. Faith is paramount to all forms of success, and maintaining gratitude throughout the process will provide an inner peace along the way.

Dedications

To Jenise Karyn Carr — Thank you for standing by my side despite my imperfections. Words cannot express how grateful I am to have you by my side. Thank you for always encouraging me to go for my dreams. Our latest transition has been our most challenging to date, and I do believe the best is yet to come.

To my mother and family— Mom, all the man I am, and ever hope to be, I owe to you because of your vision, discipline, commitment and love. Yes, we now have an author in the family. Thanks to my brothers and sister for supporting me over the years. May the bond to help each other become our very best personally and professionally never be broken. Thank you Debra, Ken and Keith for being the wonderful people you are who happen to be my siblings.

Finally, to my kids — You already know I love you all dearly. How can I ever repay you for allowing me my "get clear and creative" time so I could write this book. What a blessing you continue to be in my life and I am honored I get to be your dad.

Acknowledgements

I've lost count of how many people I have talked to over the years about one day writing a book. Finally, the time is here. I want to acknowledge a few individuals who were instrumental in helping me complete this project.

To Jenna Cabbell, thank you ever so much, for your creative contributions. You know I have a love-hate relationship with writing. To Dr. Lisa Summerour, thank you for being a tenacious taskmaster. Your critical eye and attention to detail encouraged me to view this project from a different perspective. To Ebony Flake, thank you for adding your creative style and imaginative thinking to my writing and editing. To Chris Brown, Guy Celariste, Michelle Payne, Mo Ager, Terry Judware, Jonae Helem, Arielle Davis and Jessica Velasquez, thank you for investing your time to review my early manuscripts and for providing invaluable insights.

Thank you to my former Pastors Rodney Patterson, Mark Arstad and Craig Altman for the much-appreciated discussions over a meal concerning faith, family, life's transitions, health, career, business, and sports.

Thank you to my circle of business and integrity leaders: Tirrell Whittley, Rodney Patterson, Anthony Snipes, Duncan Niederauer, Tracy Ellis-Ward, Tony Gaskins, Dr. Edward Fubara, Dr. Keith Harrison and Melanie Perry for your continued willingness to share insights, resources, and your valuable time.

To my speaking and transition coaches: Keith Carr, Walter Bond and Morris Morrison, thank you for helping me move smoothly and confidently to this next chapter in my life. Without your support, I would not be where I am in my entrepreneurial pursuits. Nor would I be as comfortable in pursuing them!

Thank you to Jason Woullard and the team at www.TYKES.co who brought the ERs to life in a very real and purposeful way. I also appreciate the great work of Sluggo Graphics who did the layout, design, social media and the website for the ERs project.

Huge thanks of gratitude to all the former and current athletes I have worked with, spanning from high school, through college, into the professional ranks, and on into retirement. You continue to be sources of inspiration for the work I have the privilege of getting to do everyday.

Meet the ERs: The Four People You Meet on the Way to the Top is a engaging book on transition and understanding organizational culture and Group dynamics. *Meet the ERs* is a parable story that follows "Eric," a former athlete in transition and rising star in the workplace who has to successfully complete a four-person rotation in order to receive the career of his dreams. The problem is--the gateway to his promotion has to go through four colorful colleagues he's been assigned to work with: Brenda, Carl, Larry and Daria and their alter egos Blamer, Clinger, Leaper and Do-er.

This book can be used to develop and train teams, groups, departments, organizations and leadership groups to increase levels of sales, functionality, communication, ingenuity, social media engagement, life skills and humor. To learn more go to www.MeetTheErs.com.

ORDERING INFORMATION
When ordering use ISBN-13: 978-1515286745 and ISBN-10: 1515286746. For more information and to order copies of Meet the ERS, visit www.meettheers.com, www.kevindcarr.com, www.createspace.com, www. Amazon.com and other places where books are sold.

PRO2CEO is a highly unique transition and business development-consulting firm for elite current & former athletes, artists, individuals and enterprising organizations that seek to increase their optimization and monetization in the business world. We help create successful transitions, business collaborations, joint ventures and partnerships for high achieving people and organizations. At PRO2CEO we custom design all the work we do to fit the exact needs of our clients. For more information and booking contact us at:

Website: www.pro2ceo.com   Twitter: @pro2ceo.com

Facebook: @pro2ceo.com   Instagram: @pro2ceo.com

LinkedIn: Kevin D. Carr and PRO2CEO

Made in the USA
Columbia, SC
24 April 2018